Did You Whittinghill This Morning?

Did You Whittinghill This Morning?

The Madcap Adventures of a Hollywood Disc Jockey

Dick Whittinghill with Don Page
Foreword by Bob Hope

Henry Regnery Company • Chicago

Library of Congress Cataloging in Publication Data

Whittinghill, Dick.
    Did you Whittinghill this morning?

    Includes index.
    1. Whittinghill, Dick.   2. Disc jockeys—Correspondence,
reminiscences, etc.   I. Page, Don, joint author.
II. Title.
ML429.W44A3   791.44'5 [B]   76-6294
    ISBN 0-8092-8064-7

Copyright © 1976 by Dick Whittinghill
All rights reserved
Published by Henry Regnery Company
180 North Michigan Avenue, Chicago, Illinois 60601
Manufactured in the United States of America
Library of Congress Catalog Card Number: 76-6294
International Standard Book Number: 0-8092-8064-7

Published simultaneously in Canada by
Beaverbooks
953 Dillingham Road
Pickering, Ontario L1W 1Z7
Canada

For Wilamet, Willy, Nora, Bucky, Gyn and Furbie,
Wherever you are

Contents

Foreword

I was delighted and thrilled when Dick Whittinghill asked me to write the foreword to his book. Thrilled because he choose me over several famous authors such as Norman Mailer, Gore Vidal, Truman Capote, Irving Wallace . . . or was it Clifford Irving? Dick showed superb judgment in choosing me because I know more about Whittinghill than anyone including his doctor . . . We have adjoining lockers at Lakeside Golf Club.

I could tell you things about Dick's personal habits that would make a house detective blush, but I won't because he's one of my dearest friends . . . besides, he has a fat dossier on me.

There are so many fascinating facets to Dick's personality and career that it's hard to know where to start. Dick is a man of parts—more parts, in fact, than the transplant center in Houston. First of all, he is probably the most popular radio personality in the Los Angeles area. He has entertained millions of early risers at station KMPC every morning for over 25 years.

That's nothing short of a miracle in a business where most careers are measured with an egg-timer.

When Dick started in radio, the only repairman around was Marconi. I'm sure you all remember radio. That's the thing on the dashboard of your car right next to the cigarette lighter. I'm kidding. Radio disc jockeys are really powerful. After all, they're the guys who built Alice Cooper from nothing to whatever he is.

Because many radio fans don't know what their heroes look like, let me describe Whittinghill. He's a lean, muscular six-foot-two, debonair, charming, and unbearably handsome. In brief, he's another me!

It's not generally known but Dick, while a callow youth, was for a time a member of the celebrated "Pied Pipers." Unfortunately, his voice was too reminiscent of George Burns' so he left. A great pity, because "The Pied Pipers" were my favorite group until I met Jackie Gleason.

Dick's interests are wide-ranging. He's an expert on sports, philosophy, politics, ecology, space travel, and he knows more about medicine than *The Readers Digest*. Right now, he's immersed in a fascinating project . . . translating the Dead Sea Scrolls into Sanskrit. Dick is a dedicated scholar. He has every issue of *Playboy* ever printed.

But to get back to the book. *Did You Whittinghill This Morning?* has everything . . . drama, pathos, humor, excitement, intrigue, suspense, triumph and tragedy.... And the second page is good too!

There is much talk about this book being done as a major motion picture. The only problem is choosing the right actor to play Dick. The choice has been narrowed down to Ernest Borgnine or Tatum O'Neal.

Even before publication, this book was acclaimed by thousands. Dick has a lot of relatives.

Dick's writing style is unique, but hard to describe. It's somewhere between Ernest Hemingway and Henny Youngman.

But in all seriousness, I know you'll enjoy this memoir by one of the brightest, funniest, and most colorful personalities in our business.

I can't think of a more pleasant way to spend an evening. To give you an idea, I got so caught up in it, I forgot to tune in "Bowling for Dollars."

Introduction

Last year, 1975, Dick Whittinghill celebrated his twenty-fifth year as KMPC's morning man. He was accordingly feted by the town, by the Mayor and at a series of luncheons. It was getting on his nerves and toward the end he was exhausted.

But there were two affairs he particularly enjoyed; the private luncheon with his dear buddies at his beloved Lakeside Golf Club, and the gathering of 800 members of the Pacific Pioneer Broadcasters honoring him. I chauffered him over to Sportsmen's Lodge for the latter, and he was quiet most of the way. Then he said, "Why would anyone be doing this for a loudmouth disc jockey?"

"Because you've become part of the town's culture and the people love you," I answered.

He huffed and muttered something.

Dick Whittinghill has been my friend for twenty years. He was the subject of many columns when I was radio editor of the *Los Angeles Times*. Whit was always colorful, entertaining, and newsworthy.

One can empathize with Whit's daily escapades on the air, and after awhile you feel like he's family. After all, when a guy goes to the bathroom with you every morning, you've got to be close to him.

Dick Whittinghill invented the morning show the way it's done today. He started with wild voice tracks long before it became popular, and he was sequencing his music long before most disc jockeys discovered how to orchestrate records and make it a real *program*.

If anything, Whit is responsible for transforming disc jockeys into *personalities*. Maybe he doesn't know it, but a lot of talented people on radio today are working because Whittinghill opened it up for them. Record players are in Des Moines; personalities are in Hollywood.

Even though twenty years elapsed before we got together for this book, neither one of us ever thought of it during any of those crazy afternoons at Lakeside. It took agent Julian Portman to put the idea together and sell Whit on it. He is very sensitive about his public image and actually is modest to the point where it becomes frustrating. For weeks, we fought over the concept, and even after the first few chapters were done, he protested doing it in the first person. "Can't you make it like an inteview? he'd plead. "I can't stand all that 'I...I...I' stuff—it sounds so egotistical."

Our strong argument was that that is the way it's done today, the personal, intimate account. Besides, his work is a one-on-one life; no one pictures a studio audience or numbers of people listening when you're on the john or fighting freeway traffic.

Our taping sessions were conducted in a little den, clustered with photographs of his celebrity friends, in two comfortable old stuffed chairs in his huge home in North Hollywood, which is maintained by Whit and his darling Willy. No maids, no housekeepers.

Along about the cocktail hour, when we had a half-hour of casette tape to go, Whit would scamper down into his dark little cellar below the game room and come up with a handful of bottles of San Miguel beer, one of his sponsors. It was the only time I ever saw him drink beer, but this was our routine. Then he'd sit there burping gently on the beer as we finished another tape.

When he related something tender or funny, he wanted it exactly right with no staging, nothing superfluous—just put it down the way he said it. It was easy, since Whit is a superb storyteller and in these instances the book wrote itself. The notes were transcribed painstakingly word for word, and this truly is Whittinghill's own story.

Dick Whittinghill is fiercely loyal to his family and friends and is admirably patriotic. If you don't like him, you don't know him. And despite his fondness for the festive life with his buddies, when he isn't playing golf twice a week he's reposing in that little den watching television or reading, and Willy is always close by.

He loves his work and don't let anyone tell you it isn't the real Whit, day in, day out, mornings on KMPC.

Someone once asked him, "How can you be so happy at *that* time of the morning (6–9 A.M.), especially when you get up at 4:30?"

"My wife is asleep, my kids are asleep, and the dog's asleep," he said. "There's no one on the freeway and practically no one at the station when I get there. And it's dark, and the people getting off don't want to talk. By that time, I'm so happy to be talking to people I can't wait to get on the air."

DON PAGE

Did You Whittinghill This Morning?

1

A Typical Morning?

It's 4:30 in the morning as I head into Cahuenga Pass.

Why?

Why have I been doing this for twenty-five years? I'm an adult with two grown-up daughters and I'm still a loudmouth disc jockey. Imagine, playing records, giving the time and temperature, and telling jokes for three hours a day, six days a week. Why would an adult do this for a living? I'll try to answer this provocative social question before our adventure is over.

I have three brothers—a doctor, a lawyer, and a telephone company executive—intelligent and dignified fellows who perform vital services in their communities. And I tell jokes and read commercials and I make more than my brothers.

Golden West Broadcasters pays my comfortable allowance, and it's obscene for playing the latest Frankie Valli record, because I'm supposed to be an institution or part of the town's "culture" as one critic who is close to this epic once wrote.

The salesmen at KMPC tell me I get good ratings and claim sponsors have to stand in line just to get a ten second spot on the program. This is good for my ego only because the rock jocks are allegedly the big stars of today's radio business. Actually, to use an overused Hollywood cliché, I've got the best job in the world. I'm out of the station by 9:15 and have all day to be with the family or play golf, and I love radio and KMPC for this. One way or another, radio has done everything for me ever since I left Helena, Montana, with a silver trumpet and a bow tie. And I don't plan to retire, which has become a running gag round town because I've professionally outlived most everyone in town. To hear the competition tell it, I'm still using a carbon mike and all my clubs have wooden shafts.

Just for insurance, KMPC brought out another deejay, or *personality*, to wait by the water cooler until I retire or die, whichever comes first. This was years ago. Every time he sees me, he tries to take my pulse.

It's 4:45 A.M. now and still dark as I pull into my parking space at KMPC, a huge two-block long white monastery that used to be a skating rink and Hollywood's famous fifty-two lane bowling alley. It has more office space than the Pentagon. Up on Executive Row, I can see the shiny vehicles of Gene Autry, Chairman of the Board, who made "Rudolf the Red-Nosed Reindeer" a household name, and Stanley L. Spero, vice-president and general manager, who is radio's greatest salesman.

The guy who wants my job, a good guy, parks somewhere in the maze of mobile units and the space allotted for the lunch wagon. When I see his car in my space, I'll start taking my own pulse.

Each day, the Whittinghill outrage begins by reading the morning paper cover to cover. If I'm not funny at least I'll have something to say. If you're not topical in Los Angeles, baby, your audience will find someone who is. I know my audience. My people are a lot like me; mainly over thirty, which annoys my rock-loving (but understanding) program director, and they run to the conservative side and like a little naughty humor, so I'm naughty. And because I'm naughty (a subject we'll explore later on) and because I recite a morning prayer and play the Pledge of Allegiance, my critics, bless them, call me a hypocrite and a dirty old man. I am not a hypocrite.

At five minutes to six, I will throw up in the wastebasket. It's become so routine I sort of look forward to it. I have a hiatal hernia, which gets angry when I drink too much, which doesn't have to be much when you're Irish. This hiatal exercise feels like your stomach is rolling up in your throat. We had a little party at Lakeside last night, so I'll throw up at five minutes to six. I have a golfing buddy who listens regularly and says he goes to the bathroom at precisely 6:05 right after my first record. I think I'll list it on our public service log.

I feel better now. Throwing up always reminds me of the day I played in the pro-am at Riviera Country Club with Gary Player. Player, who is about my size, stands up there and hits it 250 yards. And I hit the ball about 200 yards with a stiff wind at my back. So now I'm really nervous, and my stomach is dancing because I was out the night before.

I don't want the gallery to see me tee-up the ball with my hands shaking, so while the late Maury Luxford is doing his normal five-minute introduction of each pro and each celebrity—and he's getting around to me—I creep out on my hands and knees through the gallery and tee-up my ball. Now, I'm ready to address the ball as Luxford announces my name, and my nerves go like a spring—and I throw up on my ball. Embarrassed, I then hit one of the best drives of my life; Gary embraces me and we toddle off down the fairway. Throwing up is good for you.

It's 7:31 and time for me to try to break up our news director,

Tom Wayman. Wayman, easy to break up, has one of the most infectious laughs of all time. It's a daily ritual that at 6:30 and 7:30 I do something to unnerve him.

"You ready, Tom?" I ask.

"Yes," he giggles.

"Well, early in the 1800s, a woman was asked her last wish before being hanged. And while she was thinking about it, her robe came undone, exposing her lovely nude body.

"The hangman, goggled-eyed, slipped the noose around her neck, and exclaimed, 'Oh, My God, I've never seen a body like that!'

"And she says, 'It's all yours if you'll keep your *trap* shut!"

Wayman falls down and can hardly get through the news. He'd laugh in a Christian Science Reading Room.

It's 8:57 and we're going out with my favorite new group, Manhattan Transfer. Being a former singer with the Pied Pipers, I like groups that sing on key.

I never play hard rock, even though my kids criticize me for it. It's garbage and often you can't understand the lyrics; and if that's being square, then I'm square but nobody's having more fun.

You'll rarely see me hanging around with other jocks, especially the rock boys who like to be seen all over Hollywood's "in" spots making it with the local groupies and bragging about their ratings. They do to their listeners what they do to their broads.

Come along, and meet my crowd.

2

The Tournament of Champions

Lakeside Golf Club is about a par-five from my home in North Hollywood. It's generally accepted as one of the most exclusive clubs in America, but the reason I love it is the guys. It is rich in tradition and nostalgia, and, at one time or another, listed almost every top star in Hollywood—John Wayne, W. C. Fields, Douglas Fairbanks, Humphrey Bogart, Errol Flynn, Buddy Rogers, Howard Hughes (who paid his monthly dues up until his death), and, of course, Bing Crosby and Bob Hope.

My crazy group includes Forrest Tucker, Dennis James, Jim Murray, George Gobel, Don Knotts, Mickey Rooney (when he's in town or between marriages), and some of the music people such as Glen Campbell, Mac Davis, Neal Hefti, Les Brown, and old Bob Beban, whom you'll meet in a minute.

This day I'm really feeling great, I know I've got 'em today. I'm early, so I'll hit a couple of buckets before Tuck and Murray arrive—I'll be extra sharp. I put everything into my swing and hit it as hard as I can. The veins stand out in my neck, and I grit my teeth and feel like Arnold Palmer. But I hit it like Betsy Palmer. But it's straight. My good old straight 200-yarder. But today it's even straighter, and maybe I'm getting an extra five yards. I *know* I got 'em today.

"I've got 'em today!" I announce, striding cockily into the men's grill.

"Who've you got, Mr. Whittinghill?" smiles the bartender.

"Murray and Tucker," I say, like they're a couple of dumpties. "Have you seen my little pigeons?"

"Mr. Murray's inside getting dressed, and I haven't seen Mr. Tucker all week."

Murray is pulling on his golf shoes as I glide in, Early Times and water in hand, feeling as confident as Jack Nicklaus. Jim Murray, the nationally syndicated sports columnist of the *Los Angeles Times*, is a grand fellow, a big Irishman who writes like a dream and is one of the funniest men I know. He looks dour today.

"Jim, you big Irish bum, I've got you today."

"You can have me today," he says, looking worried. "The goddam gout is bothering me again."

"Too many holiday parties?"

"Oh, hell yes," he says. "You know that, plus I'm twenty pounds overweight and not getting enough exercise. Listen, Whit, if I had anything else to do, I would have cancelled today. I swear to God I would."

I was trying to cheer him up when in bursts Norm Blackburn, the old radio producer and Lakeside historian.

"Whit! Whit!" he croaks. "To the bar! To the bar! Beban is going to try to break the club martini-drinking record!"

The three of us are stumbling over one another as we race for the bar. The hell with our golf game. This is history! In flight I ask Blackburn who holds the club record.

"We'll find out today," he says, as we sweep through the door into the grill.

The word had spread quickly. There hadn't been this much excitement at Lakeside since two Hollywood stars staged an organ-measuring contest. Beban, an announcer with a voice deeper than the Grand Canyon, looks up calmly at our eager group.

"This man," he says, "claims he can't get drunk on martinis."

The slender guy sitting at the table with Beban looks like he failed the Pepsi generation. I don't remember his name and he's long since gone from the club.

"I can drink martinis all day and not even get a buzz," he says, airily.

"All right, here are the ground rules," Beban announces. "We'll have a five-hour time limit. Gin martinis in bucket glasses."

"Who holds the club record?" someone asks.

"I don't know," Beban replies, "probably W. C. Fields. I'm going to try for twenty-five!"

Everyone sucks in his breath.

"I'll see ya," Murray mutters, "I've never enjoyed suicides."

"Wait, Jim," pleads Beban, "you might get a column out of this. Could be funny as hell."

"Do you also read the obits every morning?" Murray asks.

"This is scientific, Jimbo. I figure I'll have to drink one martini every twelve minutes for five hours. I should have the record by 6:00. It's now 12:55."

Everyone looks at his watch.

"Bring us two martinis."

"Make that three," I said.

"You coming in, Whit?"

"No, I'll just ride shotgun for awhile."

"I pass," says Murray.

The skinny chap was done after five martinis, wilting against Beban's onslaught. At 2:00 one of the waiters led him toward the showers.

At 3:00 Murray leaned over my shoulder. "Whit, I can't watch anymore of this. Do you realize you've had *eight* martinis?!"

"Feel great, stick around," I said, measuring every word.

"Well, I'm going over the wall, Whit. I've had enough just watching you guys and I have a deadline to meet. In other words, I should be home before sunset."

At 6:00 Beban downed the remains of his twenty-third martini, received a standing ovation, and lurched into the steam room. By all reports, I trailed gamely with twenty-one, invited everyone to my restaurant, phoned the all-night deejay with my regrets (he had to fill in an extra three hours), and was chauffered home by a loyal, sober customer.

The next afternoon, I'm having plain grapefruit juice at the club when Killer Beban slides in.

"You're alive!"

"You bet. But I feel dead," Beban admits. "Do you know I spent two hours in the steam last night, then took my wife out to dinner and had twelve more martinis!!!"

I put my juice down and went home to bed.

3

The Kid From Montana

We were a strong, faithful, robust group, the Whittinghills of Montana.

My dad, whom I adored, fathered six kids and he was a goer. He was good midwestern stock from Indiana and was Montana state manager of the Mountain States Telephone Company.

My mother, the former Edna McDonald, was a saint. She was raised in a strict Catholic environment, but had a terrible time raising her six children in the faith. Dad didn't like Catholics. Mom had to sneak us around the corner to get us baptized.

I remember one day we were shoveling coal in the basement, and Joseph Noral Whittinghill, old J.N., turned to me and said, "Son, I think you'll do all right in business, but one thing might hold you back—you're a Catholic."

The rest of us Catholic rebels include Charles, now retired from the U.S. Justice Department's antitrust division; Robert, with the telephone company in New Mexico; Frances (Spurck), who has six kids, too; John, who heads his own pediatrics clinic in Billings; and Charlotte (Mrs. Otho Murray). And the loudmouth disc jockey.

We stuck together more than most families, and the three Whittinghill brothers once comprised the best part of the backfield at Montana High (loudmouth once made second-string all-state). Of all of us, I think I was closest to my dad, probably because he saw so much of him in me. We did some strange things together.

Dad was a state executive, so he was supplied with a chauffeur and a car. But I used to drive him around when I was in high school—boy, did I feel important.

Typical of some of our capers, we had the governor with us one time and I'm driving and our destination is the old country club where some big social event was going on. Well, the governor gets drunk out of his skull, and we have to get him out of there for his own sake. Hurridly, we drove him to the mansion, sat him down on the front steps, punched the doorbell, and roared off into the night.

We took another automobile trip that was an adventure, bizarre. My grandfather died and I had to drive mom and dad down to Pocatello, Idaho, to bury him. On the way, the old man's going pretty good—he has something in the glove compartment, and he doesn't say anything, just nips until we get to Butte.

"Son, stop here. We're going to Meaderville" (pop. 250).

In Meaderville, which is so small the town drunk is an elective office, he directs me to this saloon, which also is a gambling hall. "Mother, wait here," J. N. said.

He marches us up to the roulette table where a bunch of tough-looking cowboys are drinking and gambling, and Dad, dressed nicely, reaches in his wallet and puts his paycheck (a month's salary) on *red*! I stood back and almost threw up— I'd never known him to be much of a gambler. He was totally expressionless as that little ball spun around the wheel and me

nearly wetting my pants for what seemed an eternity. RED!!!
Dad calmly picked up his money, thousands, stuffed it in his
pocket without saying a word and we drove to Pocatello to
bury his father.

Mom and dad were exactly alike in one way, very loving
parents who gave sincere and often sound advice. They had a
"here's-the-way-to-play-it" approach that I continue to follow
today, and it has worked with my daughters, who, I believe,
love and respect their parents the way I did mine.

Old Whit is a traditionalist, but not as conservative as dad
and a bit more liberal than mom. And my kids are more liberal
than any of us ever were, but at least they listen, which is more
than most kids do today. But I always was in awe of my father
and he always was laughing and giggling about me. I think
he knew all the time.

We really had good times when times were tough growing
up in Helena. And the four brothers were known as good
competitive athletes, and we never gave up. Looking around
my home today, you see many trophies—the biggest, two-feet
high—and I did nothing but lend my name to a Long Beach
sports regatta to win it. The smallest, barely bigger than your
fist, with the bronze faded to light yellow, represents the true
spirit of the never-give-up Whittinghills. That little thing is the
biggest trophy of all. I worked harder for it than anything in
my whole life.

I was small in college. And when I went out for football,
those behemoths scared the heck out of me. They killed me. So,
I had to do something where I could be competitive and excel,
and boxing appeared to be the answer since there were divi-
sions for every weight. Young Whit didn't do badly as a little kid
in Helena boxing club tournaments and I entered the University of Montana as a featherweight.

My style? Oh, sort of an in-fighter and counterpuncher. If

the other guy didn't lead, there wasn't a fight. The Kid from Montana couldn't pattern himself after any fighter because the only fighters I saw were in newsreels.

In college we fought three three-minute rounds, and when you're doing that, you're fighting the whole three minutes— no cutesy stuff or using the ropes, you fight the whole time.

They had an elimination series to reach the finals and the championships, and by the time one reached the finals, he was really bruised up. I looked like I'd been tattooed blue but made the finals after almost two months. Some guy gave me an old beat-up pair of tennis shoes and some silly-looking shorts; that's all I had.

Now, we arrive for the big night, and I've had about four fights in three nights. I've thrown up so many times before and after them, I feel like I need a stomach by-pass. But if I threw up, I always fought well.

(In later years I came to know Cal Howard with Walt Disney Productions, who produced one of television's first hit shows—"Broadway Open House" with Jerry Lester. Cal threw up before every show that was good. If it was a bad show, he didn't throw up. The crew would run around just before airtime and ask if Cal had thrown up, yet? If the answer was yes, everbody jumped up and down with delight.)

On the big night, I threw up. It ranked no worse than second in my top ten throw-ups. Young Whit is scared but strangely confident. My fraternity, Sigma-Chi, had wagered a lot of money on me against my opponent from Phi-Sig.

His name was Zay Malone, a tough little Irishman, and we had a fierce battle. I mean, it was a *fight*!

At the end of three rounds, the referee came over and said it was a draw, and we'd have to fight one more round. I turned to my second, one Richard Kilroy O'Malley, and told him I'd had enough; there was no way I'd fight another round with that madman.

He looked at me like a Tijuana jailer and ordered, "Get out there and start slugging away!"

Well, young Whit and Zay Malone slugged each other all over the ring—it was Pier six, seven, and eight! I fought my ass off and became the featherweight champion of the University of Montana. And I got this little cup for it.

Zay Malone today lives in Orange County, listens to the show, and I ran into him at a picnic recently, and he looked awful tough—and I got scared all over again.

4

The Hot Band from Helena High

Old Whit has a musical background, and part of it could have been better if I'd been more serious with the trumpet lessons that my parents so proudly paid for. I still play occasionally, not with any versatility but loud and pretty and good enough to please the gang at our annual Lakeside Clambake.

After I had enough lessons to take it from there, I pulled a stunt that I apologize for—especially to my dear, trusting parents, who would smile warmly as young Noral Edwin Whittinghill, trumpet case tucked under his arm, scarf around his neck, braved the cold Montana evenings to take his lessons. What the little sneak was doing was tucking his trumpet under his pillow and sneaking down to Dad's wine cellar and filling his case with wine; then he toddled off to the Montana Club downtown where he sold the wine to the old boozers. Terrible thing to do. But young Whit caught it when the bandmaster finally called home to ask mom and dad where their little trumpet player was.

Soon, I formed my own band out of Helena High School; Hot Lips Whittinghill on trumpet, my brother Charles on drums, a piano player, and a clarinet player. We were in demand at every bootleg barn dance because we worked cheap and we were tireless.

Of course, we played horrible music, and we only knew about four tunes, maybe six before we quit the swinging barn dance circuit and went on to summer vacation gigs. But it was in places like Elliston and Wolf Creek that we really learned our craft. The Elliston bunch was sophisticated compared to the Wolf Creek gang.

The Cocoanut Grove of Wolf Creek was Vollmer's Barn, a huge thing with cattle all over and a hayloft and the works. The farmers here were both generous and demanding, and we were careful not to get them too demanding.

Their women would make big, thick sandwiches and beans, and I remember the coal oil lamps lighting up long tables. The guys stood around in circles passing the jug, taking big swigs. A couple of times during this ceremony, some big cowboy would suddenly hit the guy next to him right in the mouth. This was because the fellow after him wiped off the jug—an insult.

Everybody would be smashed on the bootlegger booze and still dancing when I'd timidly announce it was 1 A.M. "That's it folks, hope you enjoyed it." This was the teaser, we knew the routine. "We ain't done yet!" would come the semi-menacing reply. Then someone passed the hat. Soon filled it was with silver dollars, and we'd start up again playing our tiny repertoire (we had about six variations of our six tunes) for another hour; and now they're even drunker—and I made my little announcement again. There was another hatful of silver dollars, and the Helena High gang played their brains out until 4 A.M. when everybody started fighting. When it began looking like a prison riot, we packed up and ran for the jalopy, passing laughing and lurching couples coming down from the hayloft as we sped off into the freezing Montana morning.

And then summertime came and the Helena High swing band headed for Yellowstone National Park where we all had jobs for the summer and picked up a few bucks playing for the vacationers. We picked up a few more bucks selling bootlegger's booze, which we stashed in potbellied stoves in the cabins and sold for two dollars a pint.

They had quaint jobs for us—yard man (cleaning up with a nail on a stick), grease monkey (auto mechanic), pack rat (bellhop), and pearl diver (dish washer). The Kid from Montana drew yard man on his first excursion but shrewdly traded for bellhop, which brought good news and bad news. The good news: Part of the job was rowing guys out on Yellowstone Lake and pocketing five dollar tips. The bad news: The pack rat also had to empty out the *thunder mugs*—they didn't have toilets. God, what an awful job.

Resourceful as hell, young Whit traded pack rat for grease monkey, though all I knew about cars was where you put the gas. I had never even changed a tire, but this got me away from those dreadful thunder mugs. It was getting so I was holding my nose so much, I couldn't play the trumpet. Thinking I could fake it, it was soon apparent that I'd lose my summer job if the camp officials found out their mechanic was doing a horn player's job—the wrong tune for a tune-up.

The crucial test arrived in the form of a slick dude from Beverly Hills, who tooled up in a new Packard.

"Kid," he said, "this thing's chugging and dying on me all the way up, and I think it's the carburetor. Take a look, will you?"

I looked and I fiddled and, luckily, he went for coffee as I searched for a solution. He returned looking almost as worried as his grease monkey.

"Well, kid, what's the bad news?"

"Mister," I said with all the sincerity I could muster, "I'm going to be honest with you. If I fix this, it's going to cost you a bundle. If you can get out to Gardner or Livingston, it'll cost you half as much."

The man looks at me as if he'd seen Saint Christopher.

"Thanks a lot, kid, that's really swell."

He hands me five bucks and sputters off for Livingston.

He saved money, and I didn't have to show I couldn't do it and lose my job.

Before we broke camp at lovely Yellowstone, young Whit was to share another intimate experience with nature—an attack of the *crabs*. Don't ever let anyone tell you that you can't get these friendly little lice from toilet seats. I didn't know what they were, but my buddies, much more worldly than Whit, clued me in. Agony, pure agony. They couldn't put music to my step as I scratched and squirmed and danced for days.

I found out that only Blue Ointment or Larkspur were the cures and begged the camp bus drivers to bring the ointment from town on their next visit, but they wanted me to suffer and would say they forgot as they drove away laughing. Finally, one of them mercifully delivered the stuff—after I had tried everything, including kerosene. I was so raw, I walked like Wallace Beery.

When those little devils started to retreat, we'd line them up on thin pieces of cardboard and light a match underneath and they would scrimmage! It was amazing. Not having an offense or defense in those days, the crabs had to go both ways.

5

Hollywood, the Hard Way

No one knew it in the family, but I always wanted to be an actor, and with a half year left before I was to get a degree in journalism (believe it or not), I decided to leave the University of Montana. Dad wasn't overjoyed when his son told him he was going to Hollywood to become the featherweight John Barrymore, but he staked me, anyway. "OK, son, see what happens." Old J.N. never let me down, ever. The Kid from Montana had read about Neeley Dickson's Hollywood School Community Theater where stars such as Spencer Tracy, Mickey Rooney, and Bing Crosby had learned some of their craft. So I said a fond good-bye to the family, who thought I was crazy, and headed for Holl-EE-wood!

Curiously, I signed up at the school exactly one block from where KMPC is today. I roomed with radio's Ted Goodwin, and all we had were a telephone, piano, and a couple of cots— but this was Hollywood.

Young Whit had been in school only a few days when he met

another student, a cowboy actor named Gene Autry, and you know what happened to him. I always kidded Gene after that that I learned to act, and he learned to add. And he always says, "You did?"

Things were going reasonably well at the community theater and the kid soon discovered he was a quick study, in simpler terms, I could learn my lines fast. Big deal.

But as I'd always done, instead of setting a goal for myself I got sidetracked—off on another tangent. I met a fellow by the name of John Huddleston, who had a singing group, and I joined it and it was fun going to dramatic school and singing for our supper. So we've got this little gig going, and Huddleston surprises us with the news that a talent scout would be in the audience one night. Well, we sounded pretty good and this guy gets us a few more shots, so now the singing was easier and we became the Four Esquires (Huddleston, Bud Hervey, George Tate, and Old Loudmouth). We sounded a lot like the Mills Brothers. It was 1936.

I quit dramatic school since the money was still coming from home, and invited the other three Esquires to live with me. Now we're together all the time and singing in a lot of talent shows, like at the famous old Orpheum downtown, and we were always finishing second and winning a shirt from Frankie Gordon, which would fit one of us; and usually if we finished second four times, we had a complete set.

Soon, we discovered why we were continually finishing second. It was because of one little guy and his mother. They were following us around with the same routine. We would sing and get a tremendous ovation ("we got it locked tonight, guys"), and then came the kid.

"You got your crutches?" his fat mother would say.

"Yes, Mommy."

Then she'd ask for straw lighting (*straw* lighting) and a baby spot. And then this darling little kid would come out with the crutches and sing "Danny Boy." A little tear would roll down his goddam face, and he'd bring down the house. He'd limp off, hand the crutches to his mother, and we'd see them again next week at another theater with the same results.

You take funny twists and turns in Hollywood and nothing is predictable. Out of nowhere a slick Hollywood agent spots us and lines us up for an audition at RKO for a picture called "Old Man Rhythm," starring Buddy Rogers, the Ted Fio Rito band, and Betty Grable along with extras Lucille Ball and restaurateur Dave Chasen, who played a waiter.

We sang for the producer and later he asked, "Who's talking for this group?"

"I am," I stammered, as the others stepped back.

After negotiations with our slick Hollywood agent, the agent says to me, "They'll give you twenty-five dollars; will you take it?"

"Hell, yes, we'll take it!"

I rushed home to Starvation Flats and proudly announced, "Get a load of the deal *I* just made! We get twenty-five bucks a day!"

They went out of their minds.

The next day the Rube from Montana was even more surprised (staggered) to learn that our deal was for twenty-five dollars *each*! And we were on that picture two or three months.

A lot of funny things happened on that picture, but the one I like best is our big musical scene. One day they shoot me at a table in a coffee shop with Betty Grable, and everyone is singing. Another day they shoot a scene where I'm part of a group carrying in one of the stars on his back, and we're singing. And when the picture comes out I'm sitting with Betty Grable at the table; and it cuts to the group coming in, and I'm also one of the guys carrying the star!

We made a lot of pictures after that, and they haunt me occasionally on television. But we had a lot of fun.

We finally landed a really good job with Alice Faye and Hal

Kemp on the Chesterfield cigarette program, almost star billing. So, we moved out of Starvation Flats to a nicer, bigger apartment in town and began to live-it-up. Translation: SPEND!

On a lark one weekend, we chartered a yacht and went to Catalina. One of our group dated Lucille Ball and I had Willy —we were going together. We had a marvelous time, feeling like real Beverly Hills types. And just like always, I gave it the Whittinghill touch: On the next voyage out, the yacht sank.

Then came a stint on radio's "Hollywood Hotel," starring gossip columnist Louella Parsons. She had a terrific following. She'd shovel up all the show-business dirt, and we'd break the monotony over her insufferable monotone with lively songs. And we got paid off, believe it or not, in Campbell's Soup. And our agent got his ten percent, too. They sent him *ten* cans of soup.

It was Bing Crosby's suggestion that catapulted the Four Esquires into the really big time in radio. We were making one of his films and he said, "Why don't you guys get a big group together, it's the coming thing."

We decided to expand on Bing's idea and form a big band group, so we hired a lovely girl singer, Jo Stafford, and made it eight voices and called ourselves the Pied Pipers, which, old Whit doesn't have to tell you, was one of the best singing groups of all time.

Luckily, we were an immediate hit and signed on with "Camel Caravan," starring Jack Oakie, Judy Garland, and Stu Erwin, with Georgie Stolle's band. Our portion emanated from Hollywood, and the second half was Benny Goodman from New York and what a television hour it would have made. Again, we're living good and spending and not saving a dime.

After "Camel Caravan," through the courtesy of Paul Weston, Axel Stordhal, and the King Sisters, who said, "You've got to let Tommy Dorsey hear you," we were invited out to the King Sisters' home for a conference. What a break! We were broke, again. We walk through the door, say "hi!" to the sisters, and head straight for the kitchen. We were *hungry*. Well, we virtually cleaned out their kitchen. After we talked awhile, one of the Kings said, "Tom will go out of his mind when he hears you." And so we made a disc, sent it back to Dorsey, and negotiations began back and forth. Now, Dorsey's in New York and we're out here, and by this time we're doing well again, especially with a lot of chorus calls in movies.

Meanwhile, we're working the Tyrone Power movie, "Alexander's Ragtime Band," and we've done so many chorus calls by now I'm bored. So I make a bet this time. We had a lot of work on this picture, and I bet one of the guys I won't sing a note through the whole film, just mouth it, and I'll get paid. There were fifteen of us, and old Charles Henderson was music director, and I didn't sing and got paid.

Then we got the word from Dorsey. Come to New York for an audition—for *one* night. Is he kidding, one night?!

6

Good-bye Hollywood, Hello Broadway!
(...and other mistakes)

I'm a bit worried because Willy and I are married by now, and I'm asking her to risk our future for one night with Tommy Dorsey. We talked it over and she said, as always, "Whatever you want to do." I called Dad and said I was sending Willy back home for a short time, the group is going to New York, the Big Time.

"You're WHAT? For ONE NIGHT!?" He said to wait ten minutes. Ten minutes later, the vice-president of Richfield Oil calls me and says he has a job lined up for me in the public relations department of his company at $150 a week, which was unheard of in those days. Any sensible guy would have jumped at it. So I sent Willy home, and we headed for New York.

We piled into two funky old cars and set out across the country with very little money. By the time we got to Mississippi, we felt and looked like guys who just fell off a cattle boat. It was colder than the Russian Embassy as we looked for an inn that wasn't being picketed by cockroaches. And we found a beaut. No coal for the stoves. So the Pied Pipers broke up all the furniture and stuffed the wood in the stoves. So far, it was a class act.

It was New Year's Eve, 1938.

The Kid from Montana has his niftiest hat on as he greets New York City for the first time, and New York City greets him—with a jumper! I'm walking down 52nd Street and this guy bails out of a hotel and lands smashed up and bashed up right in front of me. I wonder if the job with Richfield Oil is still open.

We all split up and find rooms, and I'm sharing a fairly nice room with one of the group on the twentieth floor of a hotel that has long since been demolished. Later that night we reunited for a happy but tired New Year's celebration, and I phoned Willy and told her I was alive and well and I loved her and we were sure we were going to knock Broadway on its rear and become the biggest hit singing group in network radio.

Dorsey hired us and the Pied Pipers were heard all over the country, especially in Helena, Montana. Everyone was so proud, even Dad.

Well, now, it was time to move to swankier quarters and send for Willy. After all, her husband was a star!

A few days before my scheduled move, the manager of the old hotel, a wild little guy, calls us up and says excitedly, "Whittinghill, don't go anywhere tonight, I'm bringing up (in hushed tones) a *stag film*." Splendid, I'd never seen one of those things.

So here he comes, evil sparks dancing in his eyes as he sets up the projector. "We'll use the Taft Hotel as our screen," he laughed. Across from our window was the Taft's great, blank white wall.

Our lascivious little manager turns out the lights and beams this raunchy porno epic onto the wall across the street. I was appalled. Here were these naked guys running around in garters and mustaches and doing terrible things and naked broads and, my God, those figures on the Taft's wall must have been a hundred feet tall! By now, it's starting to get hysterical as we are having a few shooters.

I lurched over to the window and looked out. Here's the tableau: Here are these hundred-foot figures tangled up in sex orgies and twenty stories below here are knots of people forming, looking up at this horrible stag film, and some of them are screaming and applauding and little ribbons of people are scurrying across the street to join them.

Suddenly, the bell rings nervously, and someone is banging on the door at the same time. It's the owner of the hotel, and he's white faced and yelling as he rips the projector off the table. He's screaming he's going to sue us and to get out. But no one can say it wasn't a first for Broadway.

The Kid from Montana prepares to impress his trusting bride, and he rents a place in Manhattan's London Terrace. And I mean it was swank, a city within a building with barber shops, swimming pools, steam baths, little shops of every kind, and intimate places to eat and drink. Our apartment was expensive and we lived right up to the limits and, boy, did we entertain. Almost every night was New Year's Eve at 23rd and 10th Avenue.

The Dorsey program was sponsored by Kool and Raleigh cigarettes, a British-owned outfit at the time, and were their representatives stuffy. They would demand that acetates be sent to them after every broadcast, and we would purposely break them so they couldn't be heard—"Broken in Transit" was the excuse.

But the boys in the tweed suits from England happened to sneak over one time during a rehearsal, actually to find out if we were smoking Kool or Raleigh, and at the time I was smoking Lucky Strike, but I took my brand and put them in Kool and Raleigh packs, which was one of the few times I planned ahead in my frivolous escapades in show business.

During this rehearsal, the boys from Britain heard us sing, "Want Some Seafood, Mama?" and became outraged. "Get

that group off our program, fire them! Get them out of town!"
they demanded. Well, it took Dorsey and everybody else to
subdue these people. I guess that line was pretty dirty in those
days, and this kid knew it. (A lot of groups, even today, with
tongue-in-cheek, will try to slip something over on the public.
"Seafood, Mama" was dirty oh, yes. But I still think things like
today's "Puff the Magic Dragon" is about dope, and our stuff
was amateurish compared to what's going on now.) But we
almost lost our jobs because of that one song, which, incidentally, was popularized by the Andrews Sisters.

The British couldn't stop us, but economics did. Tommy
added strings and a guy named Frank Sinatra and could no
longer afford the eight Pied Pipers, so it was back on the streets,
starving.

We were almost ready to go home when a well-known trumpet player in those days said he would take us over for one
month to perform in the Rainbow Room. This guy was flam-
boyant and owned a big chicken farm and was a little nuts. He
came to our hotel, pranced in and threw money in the air and
you never saw such a sight—seven boys and a girl diving and
scrounging on the floor for the money.

Willy and young Whit went out and celebrated, candlelight
and wine on the Great White Way—we were working, again!
Of course, we didn't get the job. The rest of the Pied Pipers went
home, and we went to a dirty little room near Columbia University.

Every day, I'd go downtown and look at those employment
chalkboards—and at last I found one: "Help Wanted: Night
Desk Clerk at the Adirondacks." Willy cried.

I didn't want to go home a failure—all of Helena had been
listening to me sing with the Dorsey Band. I looked at Willy.
We we went home. A whole new phase of my life started when
we got back to Helena. But when you're young, you can take
defeat, and Willy and I seem to float through life laughing.

7

My Kind of Station

When I was still with the Pipers in New York, I was over-joyed to hear that little Helena, Montana, was about to get its very own radio station—KPFA, to be affiliated with NBC.

At last, the whole town would be able to hear the prodigal son singing from the Big Apple.

I heard from many of my chums, including all the family, receiving almost daily bulletins on the preparations for the big night when Helena was to go network. There were celebrations and civic ceremonies and parades, the works.

The Kid from Montana was sorry he couldn't be there, but he was thrilling all of New York as a singer.

At 6 P.M., Helena's first and only radio station would be christened.

Now get the picture. All of the citizens clustered together around their little radios staring at them waiting for the first spark of static. Well, someone got the wires crossed at KPFA and for five minutes heard the station manager's wife bawling the hell out of the local butcher for getting an order wrong and complaining about the price of his pork chops.

I think I put a curse on that town.

I shouldn't even be in radio. I'm probably the only guy who went to Hollywood then to New York and landed in Denver for my first big time job as a disc jockey. The big time, in this instance, was KFEL in Denver, Colorado—1940.

But the Kid from Montana was delighted to have his very own show on a station affiliated with the Mutual Network. The fact that I was practically in the neighborhood where it all began and commanding the night watch at $27.50 a week didn't bother me. Times were tough and at least I didn't have to sweep out the joint. My only other duty was locking up the place.

"Make sure you lock every door in the station," demanded the owner on my first day. He made it sound more important than the 6:00 news and the farm report. He didn't say good luck or nice to have you aboard, just "lock the doors."

Struggling through that first night, I almost collapsed at 2 A.M. We signed off. I caught my breath and proceeded to carry out the owner's stern order, locking every door in the place, even the john.

The next day, I march jauntily into the station and immediately sense disaster. The receptionist, who looks like Dracula's housekeeper, gives me a stare that would stop Big Ben.

"*He* wants to see you right away," she said, evenly.

The receptionist's nose was in the air as I slinked out of *his* office.

On my first day on the job I locked the owner of KFEL in his office with a broad! He was banging on the door and screaming at 6 A.M. when the janitor let him out, and the young lady, hiding her face, fled from the place like it was on fire. This auspicious opening was only topped by my entrance into the army.

8

Captain Shittinghill

One of the most broadening experiences of my life happened during the war—World War II. I was not, as some competitors claim, in the Spanish-American conflict. This experience, as always, involved radio, and it delivered me from rotting in the jungle for four years.

When the war broke out, the Kid from Montana volunteered and went to officer's candidate school, but it was perilous, too. If you didn't make it, you went all the way back to private. Running back and forth between classes, you passed a lot of guys with shovels and wheelbarrows. *Those* were the guys who flunked out! Not for Whittinghill.

When the brass found out I'd been with the Pied Pipers, they had me in charge of putting on camp shows, which was a great way to fight the war, but not for Whittinghill.

They shipped me to Cheyenne, Wyoming, and the general there put me in charge of radio. Man, this was it—no rifle, no marching, I'll just sit here for the duration. We had a slick little set-up, broadcasting from Cheyenne through Denver to the Mutual Network. We had a big band and scriptwriters. The show was called "Uncle Sam Wants You." Well, there was a war on.

There was another fellow in camp, the head of public information, who thought *he* should be running the radio operation, and worse yet, he had clout with the general. We had a discussion about our respective jobs and I really stood firm.

When I arrived at Camp Phillips, Kansas, it was slightly depressing. Camp Phillips looked like it was thrown from a speeding car. It was so bleak it made khaki look garish. If you think Hiroshima looked flat, you never saw Camp Phillips.

There were three of us there to whip a new battalion in shape; a captain, a first lieutenant, and Second Lieutenant Whittinghill. We were in charge of the army's 991st, -2nd, -3rd and -4th QM Battalion.

"Where are the men?" Lt. Whittinghill asked, innocently.

"They're coming, uh, by train," said the captain, rather mysteriously.

The men, we soon learned, were all black and were from an artillery outfit in Georgia. They had caused this little disturbance and were being punished, and Camp Phillips certainly was the place for it. "They must have committed murder," I joked.

It seems back in Georgia a couple of white MPs had raped a black girl; and the men got even by pretending to start a riot, then set up machine guns on both sides of the road, and raked down the MPs who were coming to put it down. So the army broke the whole bunch of them to private and sent them out to jolly little fellows like me.

They got into Camp Phillips at midnight, and you never saw such a sullen, mean, rotten group in your life. I was scared shitless.

We marched them up to their tarpaper shacks and attempted to sort out our happy team, but no one would talk. They only stared at us until our knees locked. What the hell were we going to do? We didn't know the sergeants from the privates or the cooks from the motor pool guys—and there were 214 of them! Finally, I picked out the biggest guy in camp. I had to do it because the captain was in his tent having a drink; he wasn't about to become involved. So, I told this big, tough-looking fellow that from now on, he was first sergeant. I don't know what he'd been before, but he beamed all over. (Sgt. Fullcher turned out to be a great guy, and we correspond to this day. He lives in Georgia.) We all knew we were going overseas and being a black company, we expected the worst kind of duty. Thank God that's all changed now. But we toughed it out together, not without incident.

Early in our adventure together, the boys staged a rumble at the PX, and Second Lieutenant Whittinghill, naturally, was dispatched to quell the thing. They were sullen again.

"All right, men!" I yelled, waving a .45 around in my trembling hand, "Knock this off and get back to your tents!"

They could have killed me. Some of them started muttering, and a covey of them inched toward me. The Lord was with me as the Kansas sky opened up with a devasting storm, and my funsters scampered to their tarpaper suites.

We used to have sudden showdowns to inspect the troops and their footlockers. Everytime we did this, we'd find 214 knives! If we inspected them an hour later, there were 214 more knives. I could never figure out where those knives were coming from, and it began to annoy me more than it frightened me.

One night I went into town to buy some booze, which bellboys at the local hotel were bootlegging for twenty dollars a pint (these little creeps all drove Cadillacs), and after getting a little bombed, I decided to have it out with my flock over their knife act. So before reveille, 2nd Lt. Whittinghill, the Kid from Montana, ordered Sgt. Fullcher to get the men up.

"Get them out here right now, never mind the fatigues!"

I read them off about the knife bit and made them stand there in their underwear, freezing their butts off, at attention for five full minutes as I marched up and down in my warm coat acting as tough as Jimmy Cagney.

After dismissing them, I heard one of them say, "I like him, he's *hard*." They actually wanted discipline. From then on, they were great.

Before going overseas, we had one final inspection. The Inspector General was arriving to make out our report card. We were ready—at least the men were ready. I was ordered to follow a map to a spot somewhere out there in that miserable flatland and set up headquarters and camouflage everything.

I marched them there like George C. Scott and found the spot on my map and was pleased and surprised to find an abandoned little house, which made a nifty headquarters.

"This is it, men," I barked. "Let's get going!"

Those guys were really fast, and I was proud. Their camouflage would have fooled Rommel. We couldn't wait for the I.G. to get there.

"Lt. Whittinghill," he said, "I've never seen camouflage like this in my life. Perfect. The latrine, kitchen, mess hall—all in the right place." We were real soldiers. We stood proud.

"There's only one thing wrong," he smiled, thinly. "You are seven miles from your destination."

What if I'd been in combat? I'd have missed the whole town.

Just to stay in practice, the boys had one more riot before we shipped out for New Guinea. All my darling little troops I worked so hard with; they broke up the place. If I had known where we were going, 2nd Lt. Whittinghill would have joined them.

Cleverly, I obtained a three-day pass along with Capt. Wyatt in San Francisco, where I loaded up on enough booze to fill my entire footlocker. So what? I was in a quartermaster company. I could get all the clothes and supplies I needed. This trumpet player wasn't going on the wagon for four years— I wasn't going to New Guinea alone.

The trip over was uneventful, except they put my men down in the rotten hold. As I said, thank God that's changed.

Well, here we are in Milne Bay on the southern tip of exotic New Guinea, the slag heap of the South Pacific, where the gulls hold their noses when they fly over. I volunteered for this? No wonder I'm a loudmouth disc jockey. This joint is at least a five-footlocker expedition.

Here we are, in the middle of the night, climbing down the ladder into the boats, searchlights lighting up the night in the middle of a war. If the Japanese had been around, Peter Potter would be doing my show today.

From my vantage point below, I could see the footlockers being lowered in this massive net and, of course, mine was on top and was starting to topple! I'm yelling—"Watch out! Watch out! That's *my* locker!"

If you know any divers, tell them there's a footlocker full of booze in Milne Bay that says "Lt. Whittinghill" on it. Tell them to get it for old Whit.

Fortunately, I was the supply officer, so I didn't go without during our stay. And then there was loyal Sgt. Fullcher, bless him—the best sergeant a lieutenant ever had.

Setting up camp on this humid paradise, Sgt. Fullcher the next morning whispers, "Lt. Whittinghill, would you like a little drink?"

"Are you kidding?"

"Well, sir, we having the makings of a complete still with us. Remember when we had the showdowns for the knives and you kept askin' what all them little copper tubes were for? Them copper tubes is now the still, Lt. Whittinghill."

I wanted to kiss him. We were not alone.

Sure enough, way back in the jungle, this little still was cooking. "Jungle Juice" is what they called it—a mixture of apricots, potatoes, and sugar, and it was nothing like you've ever tasted. In fact, it was delicious. Second Lieutenant Whittinghill added something to make it delicious.

While all the troops were sending letters back home asking for playing cards, underwear, and cookies, I was asking my wife for Kool-Aid. This pleased Willy. She thought, isn't that nice, it's hot in the jungle, and he's having his Kool-Aid. It was delightful—cherry, grape, lime, orange, and strawberry Jungle Juice. And as long as I kept my mouth shut about that gorgeous still, there would always be a little bottle of Jungle Juice under my bunk every morning.

You may ask, how could you drink and avoid the hazards of combat, the horror of war? We never had combat, and the only horror of our operation was "Automatic Charlie." Charlie was a brave little Japanese fellow who would come by every night at the same time. He was brave, because you heard him coming for miles. His plane was decrepit—coughing, sputtering, and wheezing. He must have dropped his three bombs by hand, because Charlie never hit anything, and the only thing we really worried about was the still.

I used to sit in my little slit trench and wait for him, sipping Jungle Juice. It was a joy for me, like being at the state fair watching all the fireworks.

Being a supply company, we saw no action, and the only casualty we had was when a tree fell on the first lieutenant, killing him. That's how I became first lieutenant, rest his soul.

Even with the Jungle Juice, it was depressing. How could it be otherwise? But it had its funny and warmly sad moments, too. Like Christmas Eve, 1943.

Here we are, three grown men in our tent, sitting on our cots, crying. Christmas Eve and we're on this swamp in the South Pacific, and it's raining so hard rivers are running through the tent, along with wild boars, so help me. God, where is Willy, mom and dad, the Pipers, or any fool job in radio in any tank town in the U.S.?

Then it started. Down the slimy hill, we heard one tent start up with "Silent Night." Then another and another, and then the whole outfit singing "Silent Night." Can you imagine 214 voices in the middle of nowhere singing "Silent Night"? It was the most thrilling thing. I can still hear them.

We had one crucial mission before I left lovely New Guinea—the "Great Milk Run."

One typically crappy afternoon, I'm shooting the bull with Fullcher. "Fullcher, you know, even with our Jungle Juice there is one thing I miss more than anything—milk. Cold, fresh milk. Would you guys like some milk?"

"Man, Lt. Whittinghill, the men would love it."

"Fullcher, put me on the morning report for being here, I'm going over the hill for some milk." He beamed and I probably became the first officer of the war to go AWOL—for *milk*!

I sneaked over to the 5th Air Force on the northern part of Sog Gardens. These guys had it soft; their general got his regular supply of booze, so why don't I hitch a ride to get some milk for my ignored troops?

We were aloft aboard a C-47 headed for Townsville, Australia, where they had more cows than New Jersey, and I was encamped in the rear of the transporter with a clean, empty ten-gallon gasoline can which soon would be bubbling with fresh milk for the guys back at the still.

It was about 2 A.M. when I awoke. Staggering to the cockpit, I discover the pilot and copilot asleep! It scared the hell out of me. Well, dawn comes and we're flying awful close to the water, and I gently nudge the boys and after a brief conference all around, I ask, "Can't you find Townsville?"

"You kidding?" says the pilot. "I can't even find Australia!"

Miracles happen and we land in Townsville, which after New Guinea looks like Beverly Hills. The first thing I do is find a nice eating spot and have steak and eggs, feeling only slightly guilty about the guys back in Fun City. I was told where I could find the nearest pub, which turned out to be populated by American and Aussie soldiers. Beer sounded good, since I hadn't had any since leaving the States.

Australian pubs, during the war, had quaint customs. And the Kid from Montana wasn't going to challenge them with his usual luck. The custom in this pub was to buy your own glass with the beer, and let me tell you Australian beer is about the strongest and best in the world. I wish I could import it. Well, immediately, old Whit buys three glasses just for openers. Then a bell rings and everyone starts loading up, drinking beer as fast as he can. After we're belching and scratching and laughing, everybody buddy-buddy, they ring the bell again and everybody runs outside and fights! It's like a western movie, guys slugging each other left and right and Lt. Whittinghill is getting in a few feeble licks and doing a lot of ducking.

Feeling good and toting my precious can of milk, I arrive at the airport only to find the C-47 under repairs, and it takes hours before we're ready to take off.

Back to Nature's Accident and my guys are waiting with their tongues hanging out. Not funny this time, Whittinghill. The milk had soured.

Three months later, I'm in Nadzab, New Guinea, home of our friendly 5th Air Force, this time assigned to Armed Forces Radio Service, which had just been initiated. It was near the end of the war, and the AFRS station, WVTB, was manned by guys who had seen plenty of action and had vacant stares. But our little radio operation was therapeutic for them, and they seemed happy under the circumstances. And I was back doing what I thought I did best.

From Nadzab, they transferred me to the little island of Biak, where a whole bunch of Japanese soldiers were living in caves, for all purposes beaten. But they'd sneak down and watch our movies at night, and we'd capture them and give them something to eat. They were either in love with Betty Grable or our food.

I'm a captain now and in Manila with AFRS getting ready to go to Japan for the invasion—everybody was going there:

cooks, mechanics, quartermasters, the walking wounded, and loudmouth disc jockeys—everybody. It was there that I learned about my wonderful guys from Camp Phillips. Those poor guys got the hell kicked out of them in Leyte.

A couple of big bombs opened the door for Capt. Whittinghill's grand entrance into Tokyo, Japan, on his way to set up an AFRS radio station in Niigata on the northwest corner of Japan. But first, a rest in Tokyo at the world-famous Peers Club, where all the big shots from everywhere stay. From the look of the city, you knew that we knew exactly what we were bombing and had some damn good bombardiers.

Knocking around the town, I asked a fellow officer how to say, in Japanese, "How does one get a friendly hug or a little kiss from the girls?" and I practiced it phonetically until I was sure it was perfect. But after trying it out numerous times and getting funny looks, one kindly native who understood and spoke English finally told me what the problem was. Old sophisticated Whittinghill was saying, "Where is the second floor?"

My reception in Niigata was that of the fabled conquering hero—the whole damn town turned out, including the mayor and the chief of police. They were bowing and scraping and bringing on tea and beer, and the mayor even gave me a Japanese sword. They wanted to negotiate terms over their radio station, which, surprisingly, was about the size of KMPC.

These nice people thought I was an advance party to take over their station, and I could only say "Where is the second floor?" It took hours of pantomime and some sort of translation to convince them all I wanted was a barn in the back to broadcast to the U.S. troops—and then they practically gave me half of Japan. I was station manager there for AFRS until the jungle rot caught up with me and validated my first ticket home.

Returned to a pleasant, modern hospital in Tokyo, the Kid from Montana was given a strange assignment while the doctors worked on his jungle rot—horrible stuff, which is cured partly by a wire brush and green soap. Recovering, my job was to read the pages of a book until I came to the word "scale," which I was ordered to underline and mark the page number. It was driving me nuts. But then the news came at last—they were shipping me home. It was the nicest thing I had heard since "Jungle Juice."

Just before we shipped home to Letterman Hospital in San Francisco, a psychiatrist paid us a routine visit in the Tokyo hospital. Boy, if you were casting a movie for a psychiatrist, this guy was your first choice. Two wardmates and I decided to have some fun and pretend we were crackers. I went down to the kitchen and pursuaded a sergeant to give me a large weenie, which I tied to a string hanging from my bed.

"What's this, Capt. Whittinghill?" asked the shocked shrink.

"Oh, that's mine, *that's me.*"

"What do you mean?"

"I hang it out every night. It's my penis."

This guy is taking notes like he just met a combination of Daffy Duck and Winnie Ruth Judd.

"Do you have dreams?"

"Oh, yes, terrible dreams. I'm always banging a haystack."

On the voyage home, I'm in with a bunch of nervous fellows with combat fatigue and, unbeknownst to me, the jolly sergeant who gave me the weenie has played a little joke on Capt. Whittinghill. On the ship's manifest, he had my name listed as "*Shittinghill.*" And since I was the only officer on board, "Shittinghill" was at the top of the list.

Every day, the nurse would come in and read aloud, "Capt. Shittinghill." And I would yell back, "No, no, it's Whittinghill," whistling out the Whit—*Whit, Whit!*

All across the Pacific, it was "Shittinghill." And I'd plead, goddammit, put a "W" in there.

Finally, the States! Old loudmouth was home—almost. After one of Letterman's doctors reviewed my file and read the psychiatrist's report, he sent me into the basket-weaving division for a week, despite my protests that the weenie caper had been a preposterous joke. But the looney bin wasn't all that bad because I got off every night and went into town to catch Frank Sinatra and my beloved Pied Pipers.

One night, grooving with Sinatra, I spot this bombed Russian broad in the audience and my impish humor took over. "Sneak up there," I said, "and give Frank a big kiss, he loves it." So, she lurches up and grabs him and gives him a kiss, and Frank comes unglued. For Capt. *Shittinghill*, it was my last official act of the war.

I finally convinced Letterman that I wasn't nuts, had the psychiatrist's report erased from my record, and went home to my darlin' Willy.

9

Hollywood (Again) via Glendale

We didn't want to go back to Montana, so with Willy's smiling, unflinching support, we came back to Hollywood and found a two-room squalor on Vermont Avenue behind another old house. We had one of those old cranks to do the laundry, and Willy made drapes out of Kleenex! She was brilliant. She put them together, and you couldn't tell the difference unless you touched them. But we had a house, didn't we?

Fortunately, before the next month's rent was due, I got a job on KIEV in Glendale, which became a training ground for many outstanding announcers. It was situated in the basement of the ancient Glendale Hotel. As you left the station, to the right was the door to the street and to the left were the swinging doors to the bar. I took more left turns than any person in the whole world. And old Whit was working two shifts—morning and afternoon.

The owner, Cal Cannon, liked to have a little touch once in awhile, but he liked to have it at noon—martinis! For some reason Cal latched on to me, and we had lunch from noon to 1 P.M.—and we never ate. And I'm supposed to be on the air at 1:10. After our first lunch, I said to Cal, "I don't think I can do this." He looked at me scornfully.

"You're a *pro*, aren't you?"

"I don't think so," I replied, with a nervous giggle.

"In order to be a pro," he said evenly, "you've got to go on the air, *drinking*."

I'll tell you, there were some very interesting shows from 1:10–2:30 in those days.

It had its other obstacles, too. I had to get there when the owls were still awake to prepare for the 6 A.M. shift, and it was work since I was now doing wild voice tracks starring "Granny," for those of you who remember her in the early KMPC days. Granny was a little old lady on a program called "Story Lady," sponsored by a local milk company, and she told stories to the kids (". . . and the little bear said . . ." etc.); and I took her lines from the program out of context, and had a lot of silly answers to her fool questions.

Granny's stuff and the other voices in my library were on tape, and since I was working the turntables, typing out the log and everything imaginable, I thought I'd ask the engineer to hook it up to one button and punch it up, and I'd answer Granny. The whole thing would be simpler.

The engineer made me a deal. And I'm not going to mention his name because he still works in this town, and I don't like him. He got paid extra for sweeping and cleaning the whole station. And he agreed to fix it up and push the button whenever I wanted it if I'd do the sweeping and cleaning, and he'd still get paid for his janitor work. Great deal I made myself.

So every morning I'd get there at 5:15 A.M. and vacuum the whole studio, dust off the desks, and about ten to six I was through. Then I had to wake this bum engineer up to go on the air. Cleaning up in the morning and getting stoned every afternoon with the manager.

Little did we know, but the manager had the booths bugged where the deejays worked, a regular C.I.A. operation in modest little Glendale, then and now known as the bedroom to Los Angeles. All he had to do was push a button in his office, and he could hear everything. None of us suspected anything, but one of our guys found out—Hal Smith, who today is a very successful character actor and makes a good living doing commercials. But Smith also found a way to turn the turntables, so to speak.

"All you do is take the little jack on your headset and move it down here and you can hear everything that is going on in *his* office," Hal revealed. And to this day, he doesn't know it.

Everything is going great—so naturally I get fired. Something about a conflict of personalities with the chief announcer (a euphemistic statement meaning the guy is jealous of you and hates your guts). But my firings were always as nice as my hirings.

The station manager was beautiful. He explained about the conflict of personalities, handed me two weeks' salary, and we talked some more; he's still apologizing. Pretty soon, he buzzes his secretary and adds another two weeks' salary, still apologizing.

I put one of the checks in my wallet and took the other check, and we went across the street to a bar, and both of us got splendidly smashed. Here's the guy who just fired me laughing and scratching and patting me on the back all evening.

After I got fired, I went into teaching and became an instructor at two radio schools, one of which was Jim Oliver's Broadcasters Network School, where the students really learned something, unlike some of the correspondence schools of today.

The students had actual broadcast operations. A local station and a network station. They played their own records, wrote their own copy, kept their logs, and had regular shifts—absolutely first-class training. And, as a bonus, they could do it on the G.I. Bill. And today I see some of those students as correspondents on network-TV newscasts.

Unfortunately, Oliver sells his business to another chap, but he keeps me on, which is a blessing, because even now I can't get a job on a professional station. But was it in the cards that the Kid from Montana would stay on as a successful teacher? Were the Dead Sea Scrolls hard to find?

I got fired, again. But you won't believe this one.

We had one G.I. Bill student who actually had a harelip. At the time, I thought a lot of people were going to radio school on government money who shouldn't be there—and this poor soul was a typical, or unusual, example. I mean, why should the school take money from this kid *and* the government if he obviously couldn't make it as a radio announcer? God, but he tried hard, and it hurt me thinking about why the school accepted him. Finally, I could take it no longer.

"Do you *really* want to be in this business?" I asked him.

"Oooh, y-es," he said, "I tink I cun over-cum this han-dee-cup with ee-nun-cee-a-ton an' yer tee-chung," he said, laboriously.

Impulsively, but honestly, I told him to quit, that he was wasting his time.

Well, dammit, he went to the owner of the school, and the owner came storming out of his office, right in the middle of my class, and his face was livid. Shaking, the owner handed me a check, throwing it down on the table.

"YOU'RE OUT!" he thundered, like Jocko Conlon kicking Durocher out of a ball game.

What's new?—I'm out of a job, again.

By this time I'm depressed with the fact that I'm supposed to be supporting and providing for my wife, who is home still making curtains out of Kleenex in Squalor City. Willy had a job by now. And this brave little thing would get up in the wee hours of the morning, walk down this terribly dirty alley, stepping over winos, to catch a bus on Vermont Avenue to take her to Warner Bros. in Burbank. And she'd go down into this dark basement. Willy was earning twenty dollars a week to color cartoons—you know, fill in the colors for all those bunnies and dogs and bears and rabbits. And it was a very exacting job.

Meanwhile, I was hanging around Hollywood and Vine at Coffee Dan's, where you were supposed to be "discovered," and collecting unemployment—and I got sick of it. Here was Willy, working in that dark dungeon every day, and I'm out there in the clean (then) fresh air of Hollywood, waiting for someone to discover me, like Lana Turner having a malt in the drug store.

OK, one day it hits me. I've got to take Willy out on the town and cheer her up, make her feel rich for one night. I hire a cab, we didn't have a car of our own, and I pick her up at work, and she's absolutely flabbergasted. And, believe me, it wasn't easy having your Flabber *gasted* in those days.

We go to the Brown Derby, and I order oysters Rockefeller and a French white wine that sounded very elegant. We wined and dined and felt rich for one night, and I spent my whole unemployment check on that night out. And then we went home to our squalor and the Kleenex.

Whit's luck was holding, though, and I got another radio job at KGFJ, which was a huge old white house on Sunset Boulevard and a quaint landmark for years, run by kindly Thelma Kirschner, who was a friend to radio and took in itinerant disc jockeys like stray cats.

You stood up to play records there, between two huge turntables. The house was wide open, and we operated on a meager budget and often repeated records because the library was pitifully small. KGFJ, putting it modestly, was not one of your Hollywood hit makers.

Once in awhile a song plugger would come in and hand you a record and you were tickled to get it. "Got a hot one for you," they'd say. And we'd say, "Never mind if it's hot or not, give me something to play!"

Even in those days there was a form of payola. The night guys at KGFJ used to talk about a middle-aged woman, a little hunchback, who would bring in her *hot* records and then back into the cubby hole between the turntables, where her back would just fit, and perform a sexual act for those obviously deranged night jocks.

I stayed there for a year until we were able to move out of Kleenex Gardens into a more fashionable dwelling in Hollywood. And why did I leave KGFJ, which was nice steady employment? Because I got sidetracked again by another sure-fire scheme.

A fellow who owned a key club on Vine Street got ahold of me and asked me if I'd do a talk show on radio, and he'd put my name up in lights over his place. Wow! My name in lights! The Kid from Montana's name in lights!

Respectfully, I went to Thelma Kirschner and told her I was leaving and thanks for being so good to me. "Why, Dick?" she said. "You can stay here as long as you want, you can have a raise, and you could become chief announcer."

So old Stoopnuts quits and goes to work in this big barn in Hollywood, and I'm downstairs interviewing guests and plugging his joint and at the end of two weeks, this huckster fires me. It was two weeks before Christmas and all this guy wanted was some dope to plug the place. Back to the Hollywood unemployment line, Christmas, 1949.

10

Good Morning, Clock-watchers!

Standing in the unemployment line in Hollywood at Christmastime reminded me of a similar time at KFEL in Denver. We were penniless, as usual. Willy gave me a belt for my pants, and I gave her salt and pepper shakers; but we didn't care. We were happy, and I was working, wasn't I?

Why didn't I listen to dear, old Thelma this time? Why do I always fall for some whacky idea? Why don't I set a definite goal and go for it? I can't keep Willy in this environment. Sweet, understanding Willy. "Whatever you want, Dick."

Remember this kid who never won an audition in his life? Always coming in second? OK, I finally auditioned for KMPC for Howard Flynn, who was then program director. And you know what happened? I finished second.

But Flynn takes me aside and says, "They like you here, really. So let me give you a tip. The guy they're hiring drinks a little, so hang around. You might get it, yet."

Imagine, Flynn telling *me* this guy drinks. I probably could drink him under the table. What did I do? I went back to radio school to teach.

Six months later I get a call from Flynn. The guy who drinks got a real load on one day and climbed up onto the roof at KMPC and began hurling records (78s) all over Sunset Boulevard and hollering and screaming obscenities. Good-bye, Helena! Good-bye, Denver! Good-bye, Starvation Flats! Good-bye, Kleenex Gardens and Milne Bay and Glendale! Hello, Big Time!

I was in utter awe of the KMPC staff of 1949—guys like Peter Potter, Bill Ewing, and Bill Leydon. I looked at Peter Potter, and I remembered him sitting at the big tables up front at the Palladium while we were sitting behind the palm tree.

Four blissful months went by and then something happened. You know the old saying, last one hired, first one fired? There was a budget trim and old Whit was back in the Hollywood unemployment line shaking hands with old friends, but, happily, it was a short tour. In two weeks I was back as staff announcer on KMPC, and my first job—and it lasted a long time—was to say, "And now here's Johnny Grant!" Then I progressed to doing news and introducing Ira Cook, one of the top jocks in radio at the time.

No one really put much personality into their programs in those days; they did a lot of block programming, such as fifteen minutes of Crosby, Como, or Sinatra. The guys on the small stations, like KIEV, were the ones trying different things like "Granny."

KMPC did, however, have a morning man who tried to make a name for himself. His name was Russ Mullholland, and he was making a fortune by my standards. We used to meet in the little bar next door, then called Billingsley's, and old Russ could put it down like a champ.

One day we're having a few shooters, and Russ is looking morose and informs me he's going to quit.

"Quit!" I shrieked. "Why do you want to quit? You're getting a lot of money, and you're driving a Cadillac!" He looked at me pensively. "I want more money and *two* Cadillacs." By this time I was doing a morning show on Saturdays, and KMPC was giving me carte blanche. I was playing all the voice tracks from KIEV and doing nutty stuff like touring the news room and accidentally walking into the women's john, and you'd hear screams, and interviewing engineers. But it was fun and I was happy.

So one Saturday this little guy races in and asks me, "Where's the sports news?" I didn't know anything about it, but this guy was scheduled to do a sportscast for the old Liberty Network. I do a doubletake—it's Mickey Rooney!

Well, I apologized for not having any sports copy for him, and he said never mind, just get him the sports section from the morning paper. So Rooney goes on the air, and for fifteen minutes he reads the sports news, handball scores, everything. It was amazing. We've been friends ever since, and whenever Mick's in town he calls me and we play golf.

Mullholland finally quit for his two Cadillacs, and, as a longshot, the Kid from Montana applies for the morning job. Mark Haas was running programming then, and he said they'd take it under consideration; and they had meetings like they always do in hotel rooms and all of that nonsense.

Finally, the word came down from Mahogany Row—the show was mine with one stipulation: "You can't use your name. We're going to call you the Clockwatcher. Good thing I wasn't on at midnight, or I'd have been the Nightwatchman.

Oh, what the hell, I was untried. Hadn't proved anything except it was kind of a cute show on Saturdays. As I went home with the good news for Willy, it struck me that I had come a long way to reach the top and become anonymous.

It was an intimidating experience in the beginning because

Mullholland had scripted his show, and certainly it seemed like the professional way. So, I would stay there until 5:00 or 6:00 every night typing the next day's show, intros for tunes, cues for the engineer, where to place the fanfares—everything.

I even wrote poetry leading into each commercial and wrote four story records a day of my own, and this went on for a long, long time. I remember one morning of absolute panic, after I'd been up all night doing the program. Arriving at the studio at dawn, I discovered that someone had locked the door to the room where I left the day's script. I had to make a run at the transom four or five times before toppling over into the office. I was knocking over tables and chairs and newsmen rushing to get on the air on time.

They paid me scale in those days, and it unnerved them when the show started to catch on. Letters coming in, good press, sponsors lining up. All the ominous things that confuse management. ("My, God! We've got a hit on our hands, and we'll have to pay him more.")

So, another message came down from Mahogany Row. "You may use your name. In addition, we'll give you fifty cents extra for every thirty-second spot and one dollar for every minute spot we put on your show."

At last, Dick Whittinghill had arrived in Hollywood.

Painstakingly, every week I'd type out the list of my commercials, adding fifty cents or one dollar after every sponsor's name. Pretty soon, I'm up to ten pages and making more money than the program director. I'm called into Mahogany Row.

"Ahem, we think we have a better deal for you." I was put under contract, and it's been that way ever since. I stopped scripting the show and turned the story records over to the listeners, which killed the salesmen, who said it was the corniest gimmick in the world. And twenty-five years later, I'm still three months behind in the story-record mail.

11

Five Grand for a Seventeen Handicap

Some people think that my off hours are spent playing golf and drinking. Yes. But like Dean Martin, these stories are greatly exaggerated, but I have fun playing the part for my listeners.

In the beginning, I always liked the sauce, but in the beginning I thought golf was a silly game. My first experience on the links was with my old man—I caddied for him and found the game a bore. In those days, you *swept* the greens because they were sand greens. When my dad was lining up a putt, his little caddy swept from the ball to the cup, and when he'd miss a sure putt, he'd glare at me. But I excelled at making little sand tees; there were no wood tees like today. What a dumb game, I thought.

When I got to KMPC, I finally took it up since it seemed to be the thing to do. But stubborn old Whit wasn't about to take any lessons. Same as ever, if I couldn't learn by myself, I wouldn't do it, and don't ask me about the psychological ramifications because I don't understand it myself. It goes back to the days with the trumpet. After I learned chord structure, etc., I quit. The rest was up to me and the hell with it.

So I banged the ball around Griffith Park for a few years and tried to become the DJ's Ben Hogan with no luck. My swing looked like a guy casting a fish net, even kind of faggy. Just when the Kid from Montana decided to give it up out of respect to the game, my whole sporting life changed.

Gordon MacRae, the fine singer, who was a fan of the show, invited me out to Lakeside Golf Club for a round on a real championship course. What a test! But once old Whit saw this magnificent Bagdad of Golf, *the game* wasn't important. What a beautiful thing it was! This is living, I thought, as we played eighteen, and the memory of it is vague because it was Whit in Wonderland all the way. But Whit recalls vividly what transpired in the men's grill after a hot shower. Surrounded by pictures of the greatest stars in show business and watching the sunset playing magnificent images on the lush trees and greens and in the company of some of the stars who were enshrined on the walls, a familiar face suddenly confronted me.

"Are you joining the club?" Gordon Uhri inquired. (The late Uhri was one of KMPC's all-time great salesmen.)

"Are you kidding? I can't afford *this*."

"Why not?"

"Why not?" I choked. "Gordy, I don't make this kind of money."

"Ask for a raise."

"I can't do that!"

"You can't?—you're wrong, Whit. I *know* how much money you're generating for the station, and you're not getting enough money."

"I'm not?!"

"Whit, I want you to go to the phone, right now, and talk to Bob Reynolds, and tell him you want to have breakfast with him *tomorrow*."

(Robert O. Reynolds, the famous Stanford All-American, was president of KMPC at the time and later president of the American League's California Angels—and one of the classiest men you'll ever meet. Bob was the most professional man I've ever dealt with.)

I was so naive. I lived by what my dad had taught me: Go to work, do your job and a little bit more, and they'll take care of you. Not true today, not in this market. You must demand a few things.

Reynolds knew what was up. He was so far ahead of me it looked like an elephant trying to catch O. J. Simpson, but he was so gracious, so honorable that I felt like I was taking advantage of him. I could have gotten much, much more, but Reynolds gave me a lesson in confidence. He gave me just what I asked for—*only* what I wanted.

"How much more do you need?" he asked, pleasantly.

I stiffened, gulped, and blurted: "Would five thousand a year be too much?"

He leaped out of his chair, shook my hand, and said, "You got it!" I was too dumb in those days, I should have asked for ten thousand. But, happily, the five grand was just enough to join Lakeside. My membership today is worth about fifteen grand. Old Whit recently celebrated his twentieth year as a member of Lakeside Golf Club. God bless Bob Reynolds and my dad for the privilege of being his caddy.

12

A Thanksgiving Memory

Some people can't understand how the family stays with me.
I'm always messing up, but I start out with the best intentions.

During a holiday season not too many years ago, when Old
Whit had a hot streak going at Lakeside, I was arriving home
late for dinner quite a bit, lighting up the neighborhood with
my nose. Understandably, Willy was becoming irritated, and
the kids were saying, "Is daddy on vacation?"

Here it was, Thanksgiving Day, and Old Reliable had
scheduled a golf game at noon. Willy wore a look of despair as
she made morning coffee. I sensed what was happening; the
little light bulb went on in my head.

"Honey," I said, hugging her and giving her a little kiss, "no
way are you going to slave over a hot stove this Thanksgiving."

"Oh, Dick, I don't want to go out, it would be too much for
grandma and grandpa. Besides, you have a golf game," she
added, scornfully.

"I've got it all figured out," I said, confidently. "I'll play golf and have the chef at Lakeside cook us a nice brown turkey, and I'll be home early, and we'll have a lovely evening."

Willy looked up at me hopefully, her eyes moist.

"Don't worry," said the chef, "I got a beautiful bird for you, and you're gonna love my stuffing. Everything'll be ready when you get back."

It was a brisk, beautiful clear day and I had one of my best rounds in months, and I picked up twenty dollars from Forrest Tucker and Dennis James. We were nipping a bit on the course and came into the men's grill feeling jolly, and naturally the winner buys a round. Then the jokes start, and we're laughing and scratching and having a few shooters when I suddenly remember the turkey.

"It's ready any time you are," said the chef.

Noting that it was reasonably early, I told him to keep it warm, I'm leaving in a few minutes. Boy, wait till Willy sees this. I'm having another shooter when Willy calls.

"Dick, mother and dad are hungry. It's getting late."

Assuring her I'd be right there, I head for the kitchen.

"Wait a minute," Tuck booms. "You won twenty dollars, and you only bought one drink!"

It's getting later, and we're laughing and throwing them down when my wife plays dirty pool—she has one of the kids call. "Daddy, when are you coming home? Grandma and grandpa are starving."

Here's the tableau: I drive up to the house, proud as punch, and I have this big turkey in a huge silver broiler. The porch light is on, and there's the whole family, the two girls in the back, peering into the night.

"Happy Thanksgiving," I wave, and I drop the turkey and the lid flies off and the turkey rolls down the little hill along with broiler lid and pan—clatter, clatter, clang, clang!!! The lights go on all over the neighborhood as I chase the turkey— grandma and grandpa are staring and the kids are covering their eyes and Willy runs back in the house. We washed the turkey off and ate it. Silently.

13

My First and Only Hole in One (thank God)

It wasn't long after our warm Thanksgiving memory that old Whit had one of his proudest moments—what every golfer dreams of.

I don't remember who was in the foursome, but I was playing pretty good golf at the time. On No. 3, (163-yards) I get off a nice drive, which arches right onto the green to mild applause from my group. When we advanced on the green, I start looking for the ball, can't find it. Everyone else is poking around, too. Then it hits us all at once; we stare at the hole.

I crept up slowly and, almost covering my eyes, looked in the hole. It was there! It was there! My first hole in one!

Back in the men's grill, we were carrying on with gusto, and old Whit was buying *all* the drinks (the price every golfer pays for fame) when I decided to telephone Willy and tell her about my good fortune.

"You don't sound too good," she said, "are you going to drive?"

"Don't worry, I can make it easy," I said, with all the precise diction at my command. "But do me a favor, honey, turn the porch light on this time, I had a little trouble getting the key in the door the last time."

Bidding good-bye to my fellow funsters, I lurch out to the parking lot, my head swimming with booze and joy.

"Hey, Whit, come here!"

Turning around, there sits a black and white, with a sergeant at the wheel.

"What are you going to do?" he said.

"I'm going home," I said, measuring every word.

"You going to drive?"

(Now, the Los Angeles Police Department doesn't fool around. Several club members have been nailed in the parking lot for Drunk in Auto, and a few have received 502s.)

"Sergeant, I'm the greatest drunk driver you ever saw," I said, stupidly.

"Whit," he said, "I've been listening to you for years, and I'm going to do you a favor—I'll follow you home."

What a sweetheart. I wasn't about to blow it. I pointed the Olds out of the lot down Clybourne, then made a careful left for the stretch drive, keeping one hand over my eye and the other eye on the white line. I knew I did a great job as we pulled up in front of the house. Then I bounded out of the car and fell flat on my ass.

"You're right," the sergeant said in amazement. "You're the best drunk driver I've ever seen, but you can't walk worth a shit."

Here's the tableau: The sergeant is bringing me up the walk between the rose bushes when our German shepherd, Bucky, a young ding-dong, comes running around the house to greet me, knocking me down into a rose bush just as the light goes on for Willy to see a policeman picking me up out of a rose bush.

14

A Christmas Memory

An annual event in Hollywood is the Santa Claus Lane Parade down Hollywood Boulevard shortly before Christmas. It is traditional that Hollywood's leading radio stations participate with floats, or in convertibles or buses, etc. KMPC always enters and every personality usually obliges by manning the float. Old Whit was delighted and privileged one season to share the back seat with the gorgeous actress-singer Julie London. We were at the staging area near the Pantages Theater, and I'm thrilled as she arrives and kisses me on the cheek, and, behold!—Julie brings along a portable bar.

"It's going to be a long ride, baby," she smiles.

"Julie, I'll play your records every day for the next year, you little darlin'."

One problem, though. We're clear at the rear of the parade, and it's a long, cold ride even with the bar. "This'll take forever, Julie." "Don't worry, I'll handle it," she says.

Julie swings her lovely shape up to the marine sergeant who

is handling the line-up for the parade, bats her big green eyes at him, gives him a belt of booze—and we're at the head of the line.

But just as we turn onto Hollywood Boulevard to lead the festive assault, Julie whispers, "I have to go to the bathroom."

"What?!" I exclaim. "You can't go now, I mean you can't jump out and run into a bar!"

Julie's a real pro. She smiled all the way down that interminable parade, sneaking a nip now and then and holding it!

To this day, I often think of old Iron Kidneys and what a remarkable job that beautiful thing did.

15

"One-Take" Whittinghill

At breakfast one morning I'm reading the trades and notice to my delight that *Radio-TV Mirror* says that Jack Webb's favorite disc jockey is Dick Whittinghill. Well, old Whit gets right on the air and brags about it. At the time, Webb and his series, *Dragnet* were the hottest items in television.

The next thing I know, we're having lunch together at the studio, and he says, "Dick, I'm going to do a whole *Dragnet* episode on you."

"Sure," I thought to myself. It was a nice lunch and I was thrilled and starstruck as always, and actually dismissed from my mind the idea of having an entire *Dragnet* devoted to me.

It probably sounds like Hollywood bullshit the way I'm telling it, but it's absolutely true. In fact, a couple of weeks later I'm on the air, and here come these guys from Webb's production company; and they proceed to measure everything in my studio area. Webb is a maniac on authenticity, and he wanted an exact replica of my KMPC quarters.

Then comes the script—to my house. To my astonishment, old Whit is indeed in the whole episode playing the part of a morning disc jockey, "Beetle Buckingham." Funny name in those days, but it is typical with the rock jocks of today. They've even got a guy in town who calls himself Machine Gun Kelly, and he has a mouth to match his name.

The storyline wasn't anything momentous, but it was unusual for its time and rather whimsical for a *Dragnet* piece. A girl, played by Virginia Vincent, was secretly in love with Beetle Buckingham although she'd never met him. To show her affection, she steals a watch worth a couple of grand and sends it to Beetle, who notifies the LAPD. You won't catch old Buck taking payola.

Here we are along with my old engineer, Hal Bender, who, God bless him, laughed at everything I did, always, at the studio in a studio that looks exactly like KMPC. Detectives Joe Friday (Webb) and Frank Smith (Ben Alexander) are assigned to stake-out the studio in the belief that my love-smitten fan would show up.

Webb was such a fan that he even wrote the story record in this segment, and it was clever as I recall.

Jack uses a teleprompter for his actors; they read their lines, and it's faster in series work, and I really liked it. But on the first day, Virginia protested, which you don't do with Webb, saying she knew her lines perfectly. She was proud of her ability, and this was her first part in television. Well, little Virginia got her way, and Jack removed the teleprompter, whereupon Virginia fluffed her very first line. She went back to the teleprompter and did an excellent job.

The stake-out was successful, we caught the poor girl, and the ending was a tear-jerker. When the episode aired, I called everyone I knew, the folks in Montana included.

No one is more loyal to his actors than Jack Webb; he uses the same characters over and over in all of his shows, and Jack was and is loyal to me. I must have done seven or eight more

Dragnets, and knowing my love for golf, Jack would shoot my part first and dismiss me to play golf.

It isn't generally known, but Webb is a great gagster, and he loved to torment me by calling me "One-Take" Whittinghill. I might be playing a drug store clerk and Webb would halt everything and announce: "All right, where's 'One-Take'?" I'd timidly step forward.

"People," he'd bark, "here's a real pro. This guy will do it in one take and then go home."

Somehow, I always did it and left to a standing ovation from the cast and crew, Webb laughing, as I walked out shaking.

16

Cagney and the Pimp

In 1957 the incomparable Jimmy Cagney directed his first and only motion picture as a favor to his dear friend, producer A. C. Lyles. It was a remake of Alan Ladd's *This Gun for Hire*, with the new title, *Short-Cut to Hell*.

And this loudmouth disc jockey, this starstruck kid from Montana, got a helluva part in it as a *pimp*! Naturally, I was overjoyed.

Bob Kelley had just finished his six o'clock sports commentary when I met him at The Huckster's room, the nefarious booze dispensary next door to KMPC.

"Kell, would you believe it, I'm in a picture with CAGNEY!"

"No kidding? He's my all-time favorite actor. What kind of a part is it?"

I sucked in my breath. I was trapped by one of the great needlers of all time.

"I play a pimp," I said, weakly, tossing the line over my shoulder.

"I know, I've heard your show, but what do you play in the movie?"

I'd never played a sinister part before, and it worried me more than working for Cagney. For several days I tried to assume a sinister style, you know, get into the part like a method actor. I read my lines to Willy, trying to act like a dirty little rat. "How was that?" I asked. "To tell you the truth," she said, "that's the way you look when you come home late from Lakeside." A regular Gracie Allen, this kid.

Cagney works differently from most directors. Instead of standing in the middle of the stage saying, "OK, here's what I want . . . ," Cagney puts an arm around you and takes you off to one side and whispers in your ear.

Then he sounds like all the imitations you've heard through the ages. He observed me being sinister and my lines were acceptable, but it wasn't coming across and I knew it.

"Dicky Boy," he whispered, "you're supposed to be a pimp, and you're playing it sinister. Don't do that. Smile, look happy, and you'll be much more sinister. Try it, Dicky Boy."

The Kid from Montana could hardly believe it. Jimmy Cagney giving *me* direction. He was absolutely right. I smiled and looked happy and it came over. Here was this dirty, rotten little pimp, and he's smiling all the way and enjoying being a pimp! Sorry I can't say how it all came out because I only saw the rushes. To my knowledge, it's never been on television. Maybe Cagney banned it, or my performance was X-rated.

17

"The Syndicate"

Jim Healy, the "Hedda Hopper" of sports commentators, glides up to me one day about fifteen years ago and says, "Whit, how'd you like to get into the racehorse business?

"Splendid!" I said.

Thus, "The Syndicate" was formed. Jim Healy, the town's most colorful sports broadcaster . . . Henry Slate, the modern-day Nathan Detroit who ran the Slate Brothers night club on LaCienega where Don Rickles got his start—this was The Syndicate, as *Los Angeles Mirror* sports editor Sid Ziff dubbed us. Ziff never took us seriously but duly recorded most of the exploits of our dynamite stable, which consisted of one claiming horse at a time.

Healy, whom they call the "Grey Fox" because of his prematurely white hair and his shrewdness, loves horses and the characters in racing. Jim's a turf club dandy who knows all the elite of the sport and its hangers-on. Slate, a deez and doz guy from Brooklyn, loves the fifty-dollar window a lot more than he loves animals but sees a lot more of animals than fifty-dollar windows.

Healy knew how to read the Racing Form, so he was appointed godfather of The Syndicate. After all, I didn't know anything about horses other than cow ponies in Montana, and both of us were afraid to take any advice from Henry.

Luckily, Healy was friends with one of the better trainers at Hollywood Park in those days, Mort Lipton, and he helped us acquire some surprisingly good claimers. But our first nag, selected by the Grey Fox, was an old router from South America, Fox 11.

It was a weekday when Fox 11 made his debut under the Healy, Slate, and Whittinghill colors that summer at Hollywood Park. And our hayburner was listed in the morning line at 12–1, but by the time old Loudmouth stopped talking about him on the air that morning he went off at 4–1 by post time.

We had a colorful entourage that afternoon, including Bob Kelley, Sid Ziff, and Mr. Page. They didn't know too much, either, as they all bet on old Fox, who charged in the stretch to finish ninth. It made great copy for Ziff, though, who made us sound like the biggest rubes ever to hit town.

When we claimed another old gelding by the name of Pink Coat, we ruined the act and got less publicity because he won four in a row at Tanforan up north. Then followed a string of claimers that did so well for us we weren't funny copy anymore.

And every time one of them ran, old Loudmouth brought the odds down.

Then people would see me at the bar in the Turf Club, sidle up and whisper, "What about it, Whit?" And I'd whisper back behind my hand, "Well, he's not in there for a work." I was getting to know all the clichés by then.

There was one part of racing I couldn't get used to. I fell in love with the horses. They were my friends, and then someone would claim them from us, and it made me sad.

The saddest thing was, after winning about five races for us, my favorite, Pink Coat, was claimed at Pomona.

The funniest aspect of it came when Carnation Farms came to me and asked if it could name a horse after me and I said, "Splendid!" And "Whittinghill" made his debut that summer at Hollywood Park, won his first race by twelve lengths, bowed a tendon, and never raced again.

18

Eat at Whittinghill's
(and all you can steal)

Perhaps old Whit's gambling or take-a-chance instinct comes from my father, and maybe it was manifested the day I saw him throw his paycheck on the roulette table.

I love horse racing although I rarely go anymore, especially since we don't own any nags, and we haven't been to Las Vegas in years. I never play cards at Lakeside, either, which is a great pastime for a lot of the members. Funny, numerous guys at the club play cards exclusively, mainly the older members, who relish their privacy, and Lakeside certainly affords them that.

My kind of gambling, aside from a friendly nassau on the course, is gambling on adventure, on a scheme, on something fun where we all share good times. That's basically why we went into the horse business. Old Whit doesn't expect a profit—that's a bonus—but he doesn't expect to lose, either.

Well, I'm sitting around Lakeside (surprise!) one afternoon in the spring of 1962 when my friend, Fred Lenz, a good businessman, leans over my shoulder and asks, "Whit, how'd you like to go into the restaurant business?"

I said, "Splendid!"

He starts wheeling and dealing, and he's going to call the place "Whittinghill's," and I'm just thrilled to death. Nobody ever got a better deal or has as much fun as this jolly kid from Montana.

Here's the *investment*. Whit doesn't put up one dime, gets his name up on the restaurant, plus complete say about the entertainment and policy—even the menu. And I get paid every month right off the top. And, of course, free drinks and all the sauce I want to buy for friends and customers. Naturally, I got carried away with *that* part.

The restaurant was an instant success (another way I took my own rating, because the joint had been a loser), *the* place to go in the San Fernando Valley, and the *in* spot for a lot of celebrities and sports figures. It had its momentous moments, too. The long-standing, bitter feud between Mayor Sam Yorty and Police Chief Bill Parker was patched up one evening in our jolly little spot.

The piano bar was an absolute gas! You couldn't get near it after 9:00 and reservations were a must after the entertainment started. We had people such as Julie London, her husband Bobby Troup, Nellie Lutcher, Mike Douglas, and other local entertainers at that swinging piano. The Mike Douglas stint is another story.

I thought Mike was great. And he seemed to have a steady following, and everybody was happy with him. So I go on vacation, and when I come back, Mike is gone! "Where's Mike?" I ask the manager. "Oh, I fired him—he has no talent."

"No TALENT!" I sputtered. My manager soon was gone.

Mike Douglas today has the hottest daytime talk program in television.

We had our internal problems, the usual things, like bartenders stealing from you and waitresses hustling a few customers; things to expect and things you correct, but I'll never get over the bartender who stole from me and yet played golf with me frequently during his tenure at the restaurant. This guy was overdoing it. You always let them know that *you* know they're stealing, but you tell them, up front, not to steal too much.

Another internal problem was me. Like always, I plunged into the project, heart and soul. Didn't it have *my* name on it? Well, I made a weekly practice out of touring the joint and sitting with every couple at every table in the house, and this wasn't a small house! It was killing me after awhile, so old Whit limited social activity to a corner of the bar. It saved expenses and my liver, too.

When you have a lot of friends in the restaurant business, you have a lot of tabs signed. One day our manager comes up to me at the bar and points out the alarming number of unpaid tabs. Immediately, I knew how to take care of it.

On the air the next morning, I announce: "I'm going to begin tomorrow naming those who are in arrears on their bills at Whittinghill's Restaurant." Of course, I never planned to do it, but, boy, did the money roll in! And just for kicks, I go in one evening to find out just who was behind in his bill. This should have been my first warning. But I was too naive.

Our bookkeeper, "Granny," sixty-seven years old and so sweet looking she made Mrs. Olson look like a prison matron, catches me perusing the bills in her office and becomes very excited.

"What are you doing!" she demanded. "Get away from those—they're mine" So I scampered out, wondering what she was so touchy about. Maybe it was the menopause, I thought. Why would she do that to "Dicky Boy," which is what she always called me, especially when I gave her free Ram tickets?

Granny, as it turned out, had been stealing from us for years, don't ask me how. She was a real pro. She'd make Willie Sutton look like a shoe clerk. This darling little woman ripped us off for

$37,000 and we never knew it. During the trial, she said her husband was ill, and she needed the money for his bills. So Granny did a short stretch in the slammer.

Ironically, our manager hadn't bonded her, or any of the help, so it was a complete financial loss.

Toward the end, we were getting robbed so much it became a standing joke in the local press. One guy hit us twice. Another guy had the slickest M.O. you ever heard of. He called up in the morning and talked with the fellow who cleans up (the only other person in the place was the "bookkeeper"). "I was in last night," he said, "and wrote a check for twenty dollars, and it's no good; it'll bounce. But I have the cash now, so I'll come up and pick up the bad check and give you cash."

So what does the clean-up man know? He lets this guy in, and the bookkeeper sorts through the checks. When she can't find it, she looks up from her desk, and our friend has a .38 pointed at her nose.

But the guys I could never figure out were the two fellows who hid in the freezer all night to rob the joint. The clean-up man said their hands were shaking so hard they couldn't hold guns.

Things slowed down a little at our swinging spot on Ventura Boulevard, where the stars hung out at night, and we had this business meeting at Lakeside to discuss our financial status. My newest partner had checked everything out and said, "We'll have to come up with some dough."

"You mean I have to put in *money*?" I whispered.

"Yes."

There were some fast negotiations, and my partner, who was a nice guy, bought me out.

My beautiful sign came down two nights later.

What happened to "Granny"?

"Granny," it is rumored, opened a little restaurant in Mexico with "Whittinghill's" money.

19

Say One for Me

"If you ever get to Ireland, darlin' ," my dear Irish mother would always say, "go to mass, and say a prayer for your grandparents."

My sainted mother somehow figured I'd get there, being a show business legend and all that. And in the back of my mind, I had it planned that I would. Don't ask me why. Call it a loudmouth disc jockey's instinct. It haunts me happily that I always back into victory. By doing the wrong thing, unintentionally, of course, this kid winds up wearing the victory blanket of roses. The plater who wins the derby. Come-from-behind Whittinghill, the people's choice.

My pilgrimage to the Mother Country began with a small part in the Bing Crosby–Barry Fitzgerald picture, *Say One for Me*. Fitzgerald had spent more time in the cloth than your real parish priest. Since *Going My Way* he was to the Catholic church what John Wayne was to the Flag. One look at Barry, and you wanted to confess. A super leprechaun, a giant in Hollywood's

famous Irish colony. Those tiny glasses perched on the end of
his nose, and those merry Irish, smiling eyes. And a brogue so
thick, Pat O'Brien cried everytime he heard it.

During the filming of *Say One for Me,* Barry and I became
friendly, and he even complimented me with the surprise that
he listened to the morning show. Begorrah!

Shortly after the film was released, sometime in 1963, I announced on the air that I was taking my vacation in Ireland
and invited any listener to go along at his own expense, just a
sudden whim, that's all.

The response was shocking. A real audience warm-down. Out
of my thousands of fans, three couples signed on, plus two guys
we weren't sure of, and a small covey of single (they said) young
and middle-aged women, obviously independently wealthy
and looking for suitable escorts in Europe, since they disap-
peared from the tour in certain exotic points of interest.

The tour was saved, thankfully, by my friend Bill Kennedy,
former author of the "Mr. L.A." column in the *Los Angeles
Herald-Examiner.* Kennedy was called Mr. L.A. because he was
all over town all of the time. Kennedy was the giddy gadabout
of the Hollywood high-life. He knew more bartenders than
Brendan Behan, and he was and is a delightful man, one of the
last of the truly colorful newspaper guys.

Kennedy arranged to go along on our trek to the Old Sod,
persuading his editors that it would be a fun trip, and he'd
finance it by filing daily articles on our adventures. With Kennedy along, I knew I'd have a steady and safe drinking com-
panion, and we could utilize the old buddy system of World
War II.

Before departing from LAX on a beautiful spring day, Mr.
L.A. and I decided to have a few toasts to our foreign hosts
and quickly repaired to the tower cocktail lounge with our
trailing, excited entourage, including the two guys we weren't
sure of—who ordered vin rosé in tulip glasses. Now we were
semi-sure. "Possibly," Kennedy said, "they have friends in

Paree." I nodded, and toasted Kennedy with a fast vodka-on-the-rocks. "Hell," he added, "we're not going to Russia, bring on some champagne." What a splendid idea! What a splendid fellow!

We had toasted everyone but Georgie Jessel when it was time to board, and we practically conga-lined it up the ramp into the glistening jet. At the end of the conga-line, swinging their hips like Carmen Miranda, were the two vin rosé kids. It looked like a dynamite charge with a berserk fuse.

Halfway to wherever we landed first (we had the stewardesses so charmed that we exceeded the booze limit by a shameful margin), Kennedy discovers he left something behind. His typewriter. Now, a newspaperman without his typewriter is like a golfer without his driver. With a supreme effort he'll get around the course. But he has to play fast, and his short game must be good.

"Don't worry," I said, reassuringly, "we'll get you a typewriter when we land, and I'll charge it to KMPC. After all, you're writing about *my* junket."

"Triffic. . . " Mr. L.A. slurred, and coaxed the pretty stewardess into another round. Oh, it was a joyous flight. The fastest trip I've been on, I think. But it's the only way to fly, up or down.

Meanwhile, Kennedy, supposedly on a deadline, is writing his next column in longhand, ready to be mailed back when we land. (The editor who transcribed it should have been decorated.)

Here we are in Amsterdam, Holland. A lovely city, just like the postcards. Our reeling entourage conga-lines it off the jet and heads for the airport lounge, where they are totally bilingual in booze, the international language. Kennedy dances off somewhere and files his handwritten story, and when he slides back to the bar, I have the whole problem solved.

"Bill," I said, "just relax. I've been talking to a few people here, and I found out where to get you a typewriter. Before you can finish your martini, it'll be here! Whittinghill dee-livers," I said foggily.

And, before we were ensconced in the taxi, a messenger was back with a brand new typewriter. Signed, sealed, and delivered.

At the hotel room, Kennedy sat down to type his red-hot communiqué. "Oh, my God!" he exclaimed. 'It's no good!"

"Whataya mean, it's no good?!"

"The keys," he said. "It's all in Dutch or something!"

"Aren't the keys the same?" I asked.

"Yeah, but I'm a hunt-and-peck typist. "I don't use the touch system, and I can't read Dutch!"

So, Mr. L.A. continues to file his stories in longhand.

On to gay Paree, and the vin rosé kids left us somewhere left of the Left Bank, while Mr. L.A. and I went on the town having a grand time and being treated like kings by the usually aloof and anti-American French. A good bar and a good tip gets friendly results in any language. It is now 2 A.M., and Scotsman Kennedy and Irishman Whittinghill are gleefully winding our way down the Paris streets toward the hotel, and playing an old American game—"Look-Alike." Everywhere in the world, it seems, you find look-alikes, and these two American nuts are running around the streets pointing at Frenchmen and yelling, "Noah Beery!" . . . "Percy Kilbride!" . . . "Everett Dirkson!" . . . "Leo Durocher!" . . . "Groucho Marx!" . . . "Margaret Truman!"

On a point-system, I'm winning Lookalikes by fifty points, when, nearing the hotel, a tired and frustrated Bill Kennedy stops me in the middle of the rain-slicked street, lifts up the cover on a manhole and yells, "Art Carney!" Naturally, I declared him the winner and forked over a sawbuck.

On to Dublin, Ireland!

Bill is still filing stories in longhand, and I'm the keeper of a

Dutch typewriter. And before we search out Dublin for an English typewriter, we stop in one of the city's most famous bars, Murphy's, I think. Then it suddenly hits me. My primary mission! Say a prayer for my grandparents, who were born in Dublin. And then another thought hits me. Barry Fitzgerald is retired and living in Dublin. I'll find Barry Fitzgerald and invite him to mass with us to say one for grandma and grandpa.

"What a great idea," Kennedy concurred. "Where you gonna find him?"

"We'll ask the bartenders. Bartenders can find anybody," I added.

We summoned one of the pub masters, whose whole face looked like W. C. Fields' nose, and asked him where we could find Barry Fitzgerald.

"You mean the fillum actor?" he said, somewhat astonished.

"Yes, I made a picture with him in Hollywood," I said, rather impressively.

"You're a Hollywood fillum actor in the U.S.A.?" he chimed.

"Well, sort of, but I've got to find old Barry so we can go to mass and say a prayer for my grandparents, who were born here in Dublin."

This really impressed him and right away he huddled with the other three bartenders—it was a very large pub with a semicircular bar, and the four bartenders were busier than McDonald's at high noon on Sunday. And I thought we were tough at Lakeside.

They kept pointing our way and giving the "OK" sign and apparently phoning all over Dublin. And we kept drinking Irish whiskey and giving them the "OK" sign back and having a grand time. Occasionally, Kennedy would scribble something illegible on a notepad and have another slug.

Finally, our original innkeeper sprang from the quartet waving a small piece of paper. "Mr. Whittin'hill," he beamed, "this here is Barry Fitzgerald's very own number. Paddy over there knows his gardener!"

My God, bartenders really do have the world's greatest grapevine (no pun intended).

"Now you go right ahead and use our telephone to call Mr. Barry Fitzgerald," the bartender announced loud enough to turn everyone's head.

Kennedy and I strutted to the telephone, and the Kid From Montana called Mr. Barry Fitzgerald. I was thrilled. I could feel my nose glowing and my cheeks growing warmer.

It rang only once.

The voice on the other end only said, "Yes," but it was unmistakably that of Barry Fitzgerald.

"Hi, Mr. Fitzgerald, this is Dick Whittinghill from Hollywood. I don't suppose you remember me, but . . . "

"Oh, yes, Dick," he said, cheerfully. "Are you callin' all the way from Hollywood?"

"No, I'm over at Murphy's bar, and I thought I'd give you a call and say hello."

"Well, that 'tis very nice of you," he said in that incomparable Fitzgeraldian brogue (I could hear the church bells ringing all the way from St. Charles in North Hollywood).

"Also I'd like to ask you a personal favor, Mr. Fitzgerald. Could you find time to go to mass with us and say one for my grandparents, who were born here in Ireland? It's always been a dream of my mother's."

"What? I don't exactly know what you mean, my boy."

"You know, hit the rail and take the biscuit," I said, irreverently through the Irish whiskey's haze. "Take Communion."

There was a pause. I gulped as the tears rolled down my face, and I thought of my mother.

Then Barry Fitzgerald said: "I'd love to, my boy, but I'm Protestant."

20

The Cowboy

The average citizen probably views Gene Autry as a nice, simple man who made a lot of money making western movies, who likes baseball and spends his evenings by the fire at Melody Ranch, and whose only recreation is riding Champion into the Newhall sunset. As you know, I've been a friend of Autry's since dramatic school, and while I don't socialize with him often, I'm in touch with him enough to know the truth about him.

No one is more loyal to his employees than The Cowboy, no one treats them better, and few people have his canny knack for doing business. Autry *is* chairman of the board of Golden West Broadcasters, and he *is* the full-time owner of the California Angels. And no important move in any of his operations is made without his consultation and approval.

Gene is in his offices on the KMPC-KTLA (Channel 5) lot almost every working day of the week taking care of business.

The Cowboy has always been that way, but when he's having a drink or playing golf with you, he's sort of happy-go-lucky and charming. But the thing he's blessed with is an incredible memory. Don't ever say anything to him you don't want him to remember. Also, Gene is a man of uncommon sensitivity.

Sometime way back, I must have talked about my dad with Autry while we were playing golf—about him raising six kids during the depression and getting us all through college and how he taught me how to hunt and fish and perservere. I must have mentioned that after my mother died, J.N. moved to Pocatello, to the house he bought for his parents, and he was living there all by himself clear up on a little mountain. That's all I said, the old man was living there.

And Gene remembered.

A long time later, when my dad was in his seventies, he picks up the paper one morning, and here's his picture on the front page!

And there's a story about J.N. Whittinghill and his son living in Hollywood working for Autry and how J.N. is being invited to Gene Autry's big rodeo in Pocatello.

Gene had set it up, everything. My dad sat in the first row and was Autry's guest backstage, and they talked about me for hours. And Gene personally took the old man home. It was the nicest thing Gene ever did for me.

I think the old man finally forgave me for going to Hollywood.

21

Old Kell

Bob Kelley deserves special mention in my memoirs. He died in 1966 at the age of forty-nine, and he was the greatest football announcer I ever heard. He was a great pal and like me was an Irishman who couldn't drink.

Jim Murray once said you could write a game story simply by listening to old Kell's description, and no editor would know you hadn't been to the game.

Kell also had a lively nightly sportscast on KMPC following Johnny Grant at 6:00, often followed by a recreation of an Angels' game, then the minor league Angels of the old Pacific Coast League. So Kelley put in some long, wearying shifts every other week.

Jim Healy (who wrote for Kelley in those days) and I would hang around at the deadly Huckster's Room at night while Kelley was doing the ballgames. And once in awhile we'd help him out by bringing him the wire copy.

Kell had an ingenious setup. Here was a table, a little bat and a mitt and a wire screen, and he'd create all the sound effects. The game report came over the wire in detail, inning by inning, and Kell stayed a half inning behind the actual game. He was the master at it; you couldn't tell it was a recreation if you didn't know.

One night before a recreation from Portland, old Kell had a few beers with us next door, and we had a good head start on him. We're all laughing and scratching. Johnny Grant is doing his standard five-minute monologue at the end of the bar, and the salesmen are pinching the secretaries when Kell suddenly realizes he has just two minutes to go on the air. He gulps down his beer, and Healy and I volunteer to help him.

"Just get in there, and we'll be right behind you with the wire copy."

For the first hour, we're running back and forth from the bar and the studio as the game moves along at a nice clip. I'm in the wire room again when old Kell frantically motions me to come over.

During a commercial he blurts, "This is a helluva long inning and I have a double play coming up and I have to go to the bathroom. Get me a wastebasket, fast!"

Here's the tableau: Kelley is going number one in the aluminum wastebasket right in the middle of the inning.

"Well, folks, you know how it is up here in Portland— we're having a rain squall; you can hear it on the little tin roof above us. . . ."

Kell never broke rhythm, never smiled or acknowledged me as I rolled on the floor.

In the old days, we were always trying to break each other up, not so much these days, I think, because people are more uptight and businesslike. But Kelley was a classic no-breakup; I mean we tried everything to get him to crack, but he never did. And he loved to play jokes.

Again we're in the saloon. Looking at my watch, I note that old Kell is dead in the middle of his fifteen minute commentary, and it was a big sports day, "I'm going to get Kell," I said to Healy. "Put on the radio, I'm go to break him up."

"How much?" Healy replies.

"A belt," I said.

"You're on."

I walked smartly into Kell's studio, he did not look up. Placing the aluminum wastebasket on the table where he sat, old Whit proceeded to go wee-wee. Kelley never looked up, never took the always cupped hand away from his ear as he thundered through it without a fluff.

Returning to the saloon, I bought Healy a drink.

Many times Healy would hand Kelley his script at the bar, and all Kell would say was, "Are there any big words?" And Healy said no, and Bob went in and read it cold.

Kell made some enemies in the press, especially with Paul Zimmerman and Braven Dyer of *The Times*. They were the last of the old guard sportswriters, and they resented and despised Kell for some of his attacks and criticisms of them and their scared cows in the local sports scene. They never seemed to catch on that Kelley was putting them on most of the time.

Kelley was always part of our inner circle of funsters. His restaurant, the Pump Room, which he owned with former National Football League greats Bob Waterfield and Don Paul and restaurateur Roy Harlow, was a five-iron from my joint, and you could have run a shuttle bus between the two places.

But the Lord takes care of fighting Irishman and their livers and errant ways, and the survivors are perhaps better off that those doors are closed to the old crowd.

22

The Coach Takes Over

Not all of my golf stories originate from the hallowed greens of Lakeside—we've occasionally taken the act out of town. One of our program-promotional gimmicks in the past has been remote broadcasts from the sites of some of California's major golf tournaments, such as the Crosby Pro-Am at Pebble Beach and the Bob Hope Desert Classic in the Palm Springs area.

We quit doing this in recent years, primarily because it was too much for old Whit. I have to set the program up at 4:30 A.M. on these remotes, and what golfer is coming on the air from 6:00 to 9:00 A.M.? These pros sleep, you know. Even Doug Sanders tries to get in his eight hours. And how do you expect this kid to be ready for 6 A.M. interviews after a night partying with the gang? Rocky Marciano didn't like to train, either.

Getting back to the golf story in question, it's a few years ago at the Hope tournament and the Kid from Montana is playing in the pro-am, carrying a respectable fourteen handicap, and the captain of our fearless foursome is none other than the great Notre Dame football coach, Ara Parseghian, and, of course, I'm thrilled and starstruck as always.

Well, we get together for a practice round and a cup of coffee and this fine coach turns out to be a warm person; and his parting words to me and the team are, "Thanks, fellas, see you on the tee in the morning."

Fortunately, or unfortunately, depending where the moon is hanging and who I'm with, I have a home in Palm Springs, thanks again to radio.

Naturally, old Whit has a party going the night before the pro-am opens the Hope tournament. This particular one ranks in the top ten of my best golf parties. We're laughing and screaming and hollering, and the booze is flowing like Niagara Falls; and the people and the desert are beautiful. Suddenly someone is pounding on the door; so I answer it.

"Are *you* Whittinghill?"

"Yeah, c'mon in," I say, bubbling over with warmth.

Double-taking him, he looks like a guy from the Internal Revenue.

"I represent Coach Parseghian," he said coldly. "And Coach Parseghian says for you to get to bed."

And he turned smartly and left.

It seems that the Notre Dame headman had tracked me down through Bob Hope's office, just like a recruiter sending out his ace scout. Well, I huffed inwardly, he may be the captain of our team, but not *that* much of a captain!

Proving that high living does pay, our team led the field on the first day, and right there after the second day, but leave it to one of the pros in our third-day group to shoot an eighty-seven and blow us down. But we had a good run at it and a splendid time. Coach Parseghian was very pleased with his lads, and we became fast friends.

On the final day, Ara and his wife and I are sitting in the club house having chilled white wine and a nice conversation;

and I see my friend Hoagy Carmichael and call him over, and he sits next to the coach.

We chat amiably. The coach is telling stories, and his wife is talking about the family, and I'm as jolly as ever. Hoagy finally turns to Ara and asks, "What do you do?" All of a sudden I realize that Hoagy didn't know the coach of *Notre Dame*. Maybe all he knows is "Stardust," I thought. Parseghian looks at me like is this guy putting me on? And I'm falling down.

"Well," Ara said, "I'm a football coach."

"Really," Hoagy said, "what school?"

And Ara said, "Notre Dame."

And before Hoagy could catch his breath, Ara Parseghian said, "And what do you do?"

23

As a Public Service ...

Once in awhile I'll get off on a tangent and support something publicly, but I try not to make it political; I have enough trouble with clowns who send me letters because I have a morning prayer and the Pledge of Allegiance. Thankfully, these protests are minuscule these days.

However, I carried on one crusade of which I'm proud. And the culmination of my efforts wasn't easy. Lakeside, as always, threw me a change-up when I was looking for a fast ball.

The noble crusade was to install a traffic signal on a dangerous corner in North Hollywood—where Cahuenga meets Lankershim. In those days, in the early 60s, it was a death trap, and my kids would have to go to school nearby, too.

So I get on the air and really push—I'm on the mayor and the city council and everybody. Suddenly, it begins to snowball, and the whole town is with me and writing to Sacramento. The pressure is really on. Finally, KMPC gets a letter from the capital asking me to lay off; already, I'm getting my damn signal.

What I didn't realize was, the city was going to make it a major event with all the trimmings. I was invited to cut the ribbon for the dedication of my stoplight, but that's all I thought it would be. So, naturally, I stopped at Lakeside on the way over to the ribbon cutting. Big mistake.

"Be there about twelve-thirty," was the casual word from KMPC's mahogany row.

I'm having a quiet shooter when up bounces that extraordinary baritone from "Oklahoma," "Carousel," and many other hits, Gordon MacRae.

We have a couple more shooters, and it is mentioned that I am about to dedicate my own personal stoplight at the treacherous corner of Cahuenga and Lankershim. Let us say that Gordon isn't as thrilled as singing with Shirley Jones. But he toasts the notion with another shooter, and soon we're ready to sing a duet. Ten-minutes to zero-hour, and I start for the door in panic. "I'm late for my light!"

Handing me another shooter, Gordy says, "Bring this along, and I'll get you there right on the nose."

MacRae escorts me out of the men's grill, shoves me in a golf cart, and off we go down Moorpark Street, about a five-iron from my destination, and, of course, old Whit thinks the whole plan is splendid.

Here's the tableau: Two drunks from Lakeside arrive on the scene in an electric golf cart and here before us surrounding my new stoplight and the big, red ribbon are the mayor, city councilmen, members of the LAPD, California Highway Patrol, and other concerned, dedicated civic officials.

Gordy and I bring ourselves to attention, mutter something semicoherent, and I lurch forward to cut the ribbon, kiss a few PTA ladies, and reel back into the golf cart as we sail back to Lakeside.

Imagine, we could have been the first guys in history to get a 502 (driving under the influence) in a golf cart!

24

Payola for Small-Timers

There was a great scandal about payola in the late 50s and early 60s, and it hit the rock factories hard. Some of these jokers were making enough money to start their own communes.

It was simple. The little man with the black satchel came around with envelopes full of money, and you played their records. Some of those jocks got swimming pools and trips to Europe. You know, thinking it over, I believe some of those kids making small salaries didn't think there was anything wrong or illegal about it. In any event, payola ruined the careers of some top eastern jocks.

We had other forms of it in Hollywood, too, like the "layola" girl, whom I never saw, of course, but they tell me it was wham, bam!—and the record was in the top ten.

Today I understand that payola is rising again in eastern and midwestern cities with dope as the payola. And this is a tragedy. I know of no cases of this in Los Angeles radio although nothing surprises me in this business.

During the height of the payola scandal, the Kid from Montana had his first encounter with the sneak with the black briefcase. This fellow dropped off a record with my secretary Tess Russell, along with an envelop containing twenty-five dollars.

"What's this?"

"That record plugger who just left, left it."

"Here," I said, handing Tess the envelop, "go get him now and tell him never to set foot in this building again!"

This was my first and only encounter with attempted payola. Later on the thought struck me. Here I am, supposedly No.1 in town, and the guy offers me only twenty-five dollars to play his stinking record!!!

Off to cut a ribbon with Whit doing the honors. Made history by almost receiving the first "502" (driving under the influence) while driving in a golf cart with Gordon MacRae, the co-guzzler! *(Below)* Discussing the short vocal career of Bob Mitchum.

(Photo Credit: Bob Keene)

Harpo Marx trying to get
Whit to practice the harp
before he joins the
heavenly bodies.
(Photo Credit: Eddie Hoff)

Whit with the lovely
McGuire Sisters—before
Phyllis's notoriety set in.
(Photo Credit: Robert Perkins)

Whit crowned Queen
Dinah Shore as National
Co-Chairman of the
Heart Fund, but she gave
no kisses.

Two of Hollywood's biggest lovers meet to discuss women? (Whit and Rock Hudson)
(Below) Giving drinking prerequisites to Jack Lemmon before he joins the charitable
Viking organization.

(Photo Credit: Foster and Kleiser)

Whit honored by the City of Los Angeles for his 25th year of broadcasting and waking people up in the City of Angels. *(Below)* What else do two Irishmen do when they meet? (Whit and Maureen O'Hara)   *(Photo Credit: Robert Perkins)*

". . . Sandy, this is how I would pitch to the Yankees." (Sandy Koufax)
(Photo Credit: Herb Carleton)

Former All-American football player Bob Reynolds, my boss at KMPC, eagerly lays down terms of my next contract?

One of us was sober— and it wasn't Gobel! (George Gobel and Walt Burkemo, former PGA golf champion)

Whit began the talk-variety show format before it became fashionable.

Dum . . . de . . . dum . . . DUMB—Jack Webb tells Whit.

Whit originated the dance party format. It failed. Participants had to dress up to come onto Whit's show. *(Photo Credit: Bill Bridges)*

Jayne always had talent, but couldn't measure up. (Jayne Mansfield)

Lassie was a teetotaler and therefore couldn't make it at Lakeside.

Original Pied Pipers. (left to right: George Tate, Lou Hurst, Whit, Jo Stafford, Hal Hopper, John Huddleston, Chuck Lowry, Bud Hervey)

Original Pied Pipers. (left to right: Whit, Lou, George, Bud, Jo, Chuck, Hal, John)

My first band in Montana. What else does one do in winter?

The Esquires—my first vocal group—with Ella Logan. They preceded the Pied Pipers. *(Below)* My high school football team with all the three Whittinghill boys. All stars, naturally. (Dick, first row, third from left; Bud, second row, fourth from left; Bob, second row, on first right)

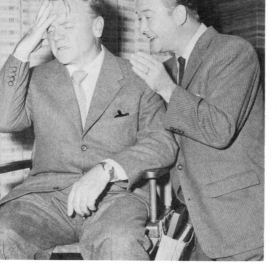

In the only film James Cagney directed, Whit tells him how to do it.

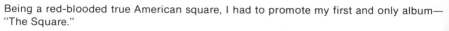

They asked if they could bring along a nice Italian boy singer. I thought it was Sinatra! (Vic Damone)

Being a red-blooded true American square, I had to promote my first and only album—"The Square."

My favorite film giant and friend, the
late Dick Powell.

My favorite employer for 25 years,
Gene Autry.

". . . he wouldn't have the
nerve to steal my jokes."
(Milton Berle)

I hate Chinese cooking. Why not Irish stew? (Danny Kaye)

Out among them one night, I ran into Debbie Reynolds . . . among them too.

My lovely and wonderful family: Willy, Wilamet, me and Nora.

ays did love a gag. My high school fraternity agreed
I did this pose, I could have all the beer I wanted. The
of a true guzzler!

What could I do wrong?
I was only 1 year old.

Forrest Tucker always enjoys my "dirty" jokes.

My lockermate, at Lakeside, an unknown striving comedian who constantly asks me for golf tips—and who I steal my gags from. (Bob Hope)

KMPC's annual "Show of Shows" featured two of my dear friends, those witty comedians Bill Cosby and Foster Brooks.

"Whit you tried. What more can you do after an eight on the first hole!" (Whit with Arnie Palmer)

". . . Arnie, please watch out for the vodka in this hole!" (Arnold Palmer putting)

Fun at Lakeside. We honored Forrest Tucker this night for his
"F-Troop" series, by drinking all the booze before he arrived.

Long-time friends, Bing
Crosby and Whit in a
scene from *Say One for Me.*

25

By the Numbers!

The worst thing ever to come along in the radio business was Pulse. Now people are running stations by the numbers, and the end result is your major buyers back East buy time by the ratings—they don't know who the hell the DJ's are, and they don't care. This takes away the *gut* reaction by the station manager.

He doesn't say let's go with this kid because he has a lot of intuition. He doesn't give the kid a real chance. Station managers are scared. They hire people with pointers who show you charts and talk about demographics. It's intimidating, rotten, and frightening. If a sponsor's product is selling and he's happy, what difference does it make what the ratings are? Why not judge it on *that*.

To tell you the truth, I don't know if I could have made it today. I know I was lucky, by today's rating standards, to have graduated through the ranks and land at KMPC as the morning man. Oh, we had ratings then, but they weren't nearly as important. Certainly, I had no ratings when I came to KMPC. When old Whit was the Clock-watcher, he took over a spot with a rating of .02. That meant that no one was listening, and two guys were out knockin' the show. When I got it all the way up to 7 in Pulse (the rating Bible of the time), then management got all excited and perhaps I unknowingly contributed to the numbers game.

In the early days, I liked to go out and mingle with the people and find out who my audience was. And mine is beautiful—sixteen on up. I still get a whole bunch of story records from kids twelve to sixteen. One girl in senior high is a constant contributor, and the guys in the chart room with the demographics say there's no such person listening to my show. My audience is supposed to be thirty to forty-nine. Horse pucky.

In the late 50s our all-night man, John McShane, was interviewed at home by Pulse; one of the only guys I ever knew who was interviewed. The interviewer sat down and asked him questions about his family, what kind of car he drives and his income, etc. "And what radio station do you listen to?" the interviewer finally asked.

"I only listen to KMPC," said McShane, triumphantly.

And the interviewer said, get *this*, "Oh, c'mon, now, everybody listens to KFWB!"

"Well *I* listen to KMPC!" McShane, shot back, testily.

"That can't be right, everybody on the block listens to KFWB."

Now, of course, the interviewer goes back to the office and says KFWB looks awfully good.

You know what produces good ratings. Innovators. The guys who create. The best program director I ever worked for was Bob Forward, now a successful actor. Forward invented the mobile unit traffic helicopter and emergency service, which has been copied by almost every major station in the United States. Forward also had faith in his talent and pushed to get the best out of them. What he did for Los Angeles radio can never be repaid to him.

Another facet of ratings that drives me up the wall is the telephone survey. Usually, this poll is taken between three and six in the afternoon when adults are working, so who answers? —the kids. Well, the kids are going to name their favorite rock station, and boom! this goes down in the figures. And all the Fred Frenetics in town run to their favorite Hollywood hangout and show their numbers around. There has to be a better way.

Salesmen used to go out and sell a program or a fellow, but they don't have to do that anymore—just show the little book with the figures. They're only selling time, not talent.

I don't look at the ratings. If I come in in the morning, and the station log is filled with commercials, I *know* I have another day.

26

Program Directors
(...the phoniest job in radio)

The other day, I played a new Frank Sinatra record, "Empty Tables," which I think is a Sinatra classic. A beautiful lyric, lush orchestration by Gordon Jenkins, and Sinatra at his controlled best—the phrasing, impeccable.

I was told the record was a "tune out," and that it was off the station's playlist because it wouldn't appeal to the 25–49 age group. Bullshit! It got me to thinking about program directors, again. I've always had trouble with them. And call it egotistical, but in every instance I thought I knew more than they did.

I've been battling with them ever since I was fired from KFEL in Denver. (And that's a quick story: We were putting on a play about Abraham Lincoln, and no one could find the program director for two days. So I volunteered to direct it. Also, I made a few changes in the script, and it came off nicely. But the program director shows up the next day and fires me for directing the play, saying it was his job.)

Program directors are a necessary evil who are, in reality, front men for the sales department and the guys who claim to know how to read the ratings.

It's a self-perpetuating job, and they do things that are sort of a job justification, like they say in the army, "Make your own job." Some of their more important functions are to put up notices and signs on bulletin boards, send out memos to the jocks and type up the station's playlist, and make sure the jocks are following their little card index of what to play.

Not long ago I told a former program director that I have musical integrity, and that his ilk did not. And he agreed. "We program music for the mass audience," he said. "We have no musical integrity."

One of my competing colleagues one day got on the air and was kidding around about Federal Communications Commission (FCC) rules and license renewals and wondered aloud, "Does the FCC require that I have to play the same record every hour?" Well, the program director (p.d.) came storming into his office after his program and they had a pip of an argument. My colleague finished up his rebuttal by throwing a stack of records at the p.d. and telling him to shove them up his ass! I had new respect for my fellow disc jockey after that.

I've always believed that a disc jockey should have a musical background. And if he doesn't, what kind of help can a p.d. give him when some p.d.'s have tin ears? There are a couple of deejays in this town, besides myself, who have musical training and knowledge and know how to sequence and are able to impart some wisdom and insight about the music they're playing. Paul Compton of KRLA is one and so is Chuck Southcott, now with Radio Arts, which syndicates the only adult "top 40" I know of.

Another thing I'm sick of is the "entity factor." The overall "sound syndrome." Some p.d.'s will say we're not sounding like one thing, we're sounding like we're jumbled up. So what the hell's wrong with that? You get a bunch of good jocks together who know music and select their own stuff, and you get the best kind of programming—diversified and professional.

I play good music and a few of the good new tunes, but don't ever let a program director tell me I'm "tuning out" the 25–49 group with Sinatra or Como or Peggy Lee or Duke Ellington.

It pains me that a whole generation of kids have grown up never having heard any good music. Since I first played "Sh-Boom" back in the 50s, the kids have heard nothing but these rock groups who sing out of key (a few sing on key, I know). And on stage they can't sing or move around, and eventually most of them drop out of the scene.

Imagine, a whole generation hearing nothing more than two chords, not being exposed to real good music.

There is one rock critic in this town who is so enamored of his role that he once wrote that Elvis Presley, who can *sing*, should retire because he hasn't *progressed* in twenty years. Progressed? What the hell is he supposed to do? He's Elvis Presley. Like Bing is Bing and Frank is Frank! What progressed? This critic would make a good program director.

I recall a classic story about how one of Hollywood's highest-rated rock stations became a rocker. It was during the time that rock 'n' roll was really big. Well, the station's ratings were poor, mainly due to so many changes in personalities. So, the station throws a cocktail party for its new eastern owners, and the p.d. goes up to the president of the chain and asks how the ratings could be improved? The eastern executive downed the remainder of his martini and said coldly, "Rock the son-of-a-bitch." Isn't that suave? That's how rock stations are born. Or, when in doubt, rock it.

Whenever I have the occasion to converse with one of the rock p.d.'s, which, happily, is rarely, they talk to me like I'm some kind of Martian. They talk about cumes and demographics and identity factors and the target audience, and a lot of them are overage phonies with long hair, playing the role for their target audience, and who couldn't get a job outside of radio. And most of them talk their way into radio after establishing some sort of track record with advertising agencies, or perhaps they're related to the owner of the company.

One of my favorite pastimes in the old days, I'm admitting for the first time here, was tearing down some idiotic memo the p.d. had put up on the bulletin board. I was also one of the guys who taped up a story attacking certain programming policies.

I've noticed that two stations in Hollywood have made a huge jump into the top ten–rated outlets, and it's scaring some people because these stations are both FM and both play beautiful music. And I also noticed very few rock nominees in the recent Grammy nominations. Is there evidence of a new trend back to good music, at last? What, pray tell, will our learned program directors do if *this* happens? They might have to ask us *old guys* what to do? And they'd be out of a job. But let me make one thing perfectly clear—I've never met any of these program directors at KMPC.

27

Tales of the Lakeside Woods
(...and other fables)

When I was a little kid in Montana, I never dreamed of anything like Lakeside Golf Club. And when I was a nobody disc jockey in exotic Glendale, I never dreamed of having a locker next to Bob Hope.

I never dreamed of Bing Crosby saying "Hi" to me and, to this day saying, "Dick, you still got that three-hour mornin' thing going?" I'm in awe of it, the whole thing, all the elements. Like, being buddies with Forrest Tucker and Foster Brooks and having them on my program—what an honor. But they're just like you and me in one respect. They *worked* to get there.

Since 1957 Bob Hope and I have been telling each other jokes in our little cubbyhole in the locker room. In all those years, he's told me three stories I've never heard, and I've told him two he's never heard. Five jokes in almost twenty years! But he's the greatest audience in the world. Tell him a funny joke, and he bangs his locker and falls down. And once this little Kid from Montana told Bob Hope a joke that he actually used on his television show. Bob Hope used *my* joke. I was never so honored in my life.

Here it is, but try to imagine Hope telling it:

> The army is staging maneuvers, but decides no arms will be used in the modern army, but it will have regular rules.
>
> When the red division stages a mock battle with the blue division, whoever says "Bang, Bang!" first shoots the other guy dead. "What happens if the guy keeps coming when you say Bang, Bang? " a recruit asks.
>
> Then you take out an imaginary knife and say, "Cut, Cut!"
>
> So, the recruit goes out and confronts a member of the enemy and yells, "Bang, Bang!" But the enemy keeps advancing.
>
> And again he yells, "Bang, Bang!" And the enemy keeps coming.
>
> "Cut, cut!" he yells. "Cut, Cut!"
>
> And the other guy pushes him over and knocks him flat on his back.
>
> "Tank, Tank!" says the other guy.

Hope gave it a swishy ending, and it got a big laugh on the program.

Mickey Rooney was kicked out of the club years ago for allegedly ripping up a drinking fountain that wouldn't work and pitching it into the L.A. River. Well, whatever the reason, he comes by to play golf with me as my guest. Mickey Rooney—as *my* guest!

Rooney is a darling little man who drives me up the pine trees on the course. He keeps up a constant stream of chatter and corrects every move I make. He calls me everything but my right name and sometimes I wonder if he really knows it.

"Whickledickle," he'll say, "turn your left toe slightly toward the ball when you hit that iron. . . ." "Whittledooper, bring that club head back farther and flatter when you start your backswing. . . ." "Whifflepooper, don't do that, stand right over your putt. . . ."

By the time we get to the back nine, I'm so nervous I want to quit. But Mick's funny, too. Sometimes he'll act out a whole screenplay he claims he's written, but I suspect he makes it up along the way.

Right in the middle of a crucial shot, especially if someone new is in the foursome, he'll suddenly say aloud, "You know, I was six-foot-four the night I married Ava Gardner, and when I woke up in the morning, someone cut my legs off."

Once I asked him why so many marriages? And he said, "Every time I get married, I'm in love. But after awhile she's my mother." Mickey didn't smile when he said it, either.

And what an athlete he is. That little bull gets up there and hits the ball 230 yards.

I love it when out of the blue, maybe after a year, he'll call me on my private line at seven in the morning and chirp, "Whiddlefiddle, let's play golf!"

George Gobel is very serious on the course, but he's known to have a little touch, and when he has too many touches, he mumbles. He has a friend who mumbles, too, and when they get together in the men's grill, you can't understand a thing they're saying.

One day Gobel is mumbling more than usual and lurching a bit. And we're talking, and he doesn't make any sense. So I say to him, "George, I'm driving you home." And I take him by the arm, still mumbling, and drive him all the way home.

Spooky old Alice comes to the door (there *really* is an Alice) and slams it in our face. Finally, we get in, and George leads me right to the billiard room, hands me a stick, and says, perfectly coherently, "Let's play." Well, he beats the hell out of me. All the time, he was pretending to be tighter than he was. He's done that twice to me.

Forrest Tucker is the last of his breed in films. The only other actor, physically, I compare him to is the late Victor McLaglen. Tuck, however, is more versatile because he's an exceptional song and dance man. And he's also a big, loudmouth, happy Irishman, and he does as much or more for his fellowman than Frank Sinatra.

Tuck is a fine golfer, one of the best in the film colony, and when he hits it off the tee it rockets down the fairway. Just like the rest of us, Tuck nips a wee bit and it's a rather washy eighteen when we Irish are together.

Tuck used to go a little harder than he does these days ("I take six weeks off a year for my liver") when he went around Lakeside in his famous "F Troop" golfcart. It was complete with a portable television set, radio, and a fully stocked bar with ice and cups. He'd take it to the studio with him and drive it home from the course since he lives right off the eleventh green on Golfball Row.

I haven't seen the little booze wagon in some time, and I suspect Tuck has it in his garage because every freeloader at Lakeside was depleting his portable bar at an embarrassing rate.

Tuck has been involved in many legendary golf matches, and some years ago in a contest with Johnny Weissmuller, the famous Tarzan of the movies, he finished head to head with one of the greatest putts ever seen at Lakeside.

Forrie and Norm Blackburn also helped put March Air Force base on the map when they volunteered to help bring a group of stars down there for a benefit tournament and, as always, Tuck was the first one there getting everything ready.

Every year when I go on vacation, Tuck is one of the guests who sits in for me and does the best job of anyone. He loves doing it and right up front he tells the audience he starts the program off with a little belt. When Forrest Tucker is in town, he always tells my friends, he doesn't feel right if he doesn't begin each day with my program. He's so Irish and so kind.

Foster Brooks is a loyal friend. No matter where he's appearing, he comes in once a month to record comedy spots with me. I asked why he does this, since he's making big money, and he does those bits for me for scale.

"I'll tell you why," he said, "you helped me when I needed it." Actually, Perry Como was responsible for Foster's success, bringing him to Las Vegas as part of Perry's show.

The first time I saw Foster doing his drunk act I fell flat on my face. What's this guy doing at forty-eight-years-old not working? We wanted to get him some exposure, so we got him to do a few local things for important people. I remember setting him up for a whole convention of doctors who were having their golf tournament dinner at Lakeside. We brought Foster up to the dais and introduced him as a prominent brain surgeon from Detroit.

Well, Foster began rather learnedly, acting, of course, like he's a little smashed but trying not to show it. The guys who know are watching the doctors' expressions, first puzzled, then quizical, then baffled—and we're dying.

Now he's acting drunker and drunker. He starts a discourse on his recent operation, brain surgery on the famous Beverly Hills attorney, Paul Caruso.

"I—I—I opend-dup h-h-h-is skul-ull, t-took one l-look, and sl-lammed it shut!"

Now the doctors are going crazy, finally catching on.

To give you an idea what his peers think of him now, Bob Hope won't follow Foster Brooks and openly says so.

And my Italian drinking buddy, Demi Sposa, better known to audiences everywhere as Dennis James, who is absolutely the greatest TV emcee in the world. Dennis has probably done more to improve my golf game than any of the pseudo pros at Lakeside. Aside from the fact that he drinks scotch and Calso water, he's a terrific person. And if he ever bets you he can hit a ball farther left-handed than you can with both hands—don't bet him.

We have fun, but we don't do the crazy things the old crowd pulled, guys like W. C. Fields, Oliver Hardy, and Johnny Weissmuller. Fields, I'm told, sometimes got drunk and fired a shotgun at the swans on Toluca Lake, and Weissmuller, whom I've played with often, used to pick guys up and stuff them in their lockers. And then he'd get loaded and go home at two in the morning (he lived right behind the course) and let out his Tarzan yell and watch all the lights go on in North Hollywood.

One year we had a Roaring Twenties Golf Tournament open only to guys who were horrible golfers up to thirty handicap. It was bad enough having a handicap that high, but we'd also try to ruin their games; on one green we'd have a huge hole and on another a tiny one, things like that.

Gobel and I were riding around the course wearing pith helmets and carrying shotguns, and we weren't in golf carts—we were riding camels! Our instructions were to sneak up on these guys (how do you sneak up on someone on a camel?), and when they'd start to swing, shoot off the guns. Would they jump!

We were really getting into it, and George and I conspired for what we thought was the biggest gag of all. We tethered the camels out of sight and sneaked up on this foursome, which included a guest with the worst swing I'd ever seen in my life. "OK, Georgie, when he takes his backswing, we both shoot our shotguns off together." Gobel squealed with delight.

This particular guest had a swing like an octopus falling out of a tree, and he took back with the club and BLAM!—you never heard such a noise. This poor fellow jumps six feet in the air and, I swear, gets a hole in one!

Then we find out there was no prize for a hole in one, I mean, who expected it from this bunch of hackers? So Jim Cross, the Oldsmobile dealer, goes out scouting for a car and returns with an old used one, but at least the guy got a car. After all, he could have had a coronary.

Another fine afternoon I'm in a foursome with Tuck, and we're waiting for the fourth guy, who is in the bar having some shooters. Tuck is upset by the time the fellow catches up to us.

"You're holding us up," Tuck said. "Take your Mulligan on any hole," he added, gruffly. (For those of you who don't know, a *Mulligan* is a second shot off the tee after you've messed up your first drive. You get only one freebie, or Mulligan.)

We're halfway around the course on a little par-three, and this chap hits a drive that bounces off the trees, and he immediately screams, "That's my Mulligan!"—and the ball skirts the trap and caroms off a rake for a hole in one.

"I got a hole in one, I got a hole in one!" The guy is dancing. Tuck studies him coolly.

"Take another shot, baby, that's your Mulligan."

One of my favorite golf stories involves Perry Como, a sweet, charming man. We had just finished nine holes one day, and he was as relaxed as you see him on TV and telling jokes when someone rushes up with the news that one of my daughters has had an accident. He didn't even know which daughter. Well, I dashed over to the emergency hospital, and there was Willy. She had fallen out of a tree and broken her wrist (it's not exactly a hilarious golf story).

That evening we're all consoling her when I get a phone call from Perry Como, who stopped off to find out how my daughter was while on his way to rehearsals at NBC. It touched me, and Willy never forgot it.

In the late fifties I was privileged to host TV's first golf series with the great Arnold Palmer and Gary Player. Dick Irving, the producer, was a fan of the program, and he knew where to find me—at Lakeside. So he caught me in the men's grill and asked me if I would do it, and I said, "Splendid."

It was called "Challenge Golf" for ABC. And Irving had this small problem: He did not know anything about golf, but he had a good director, Jim Bowers, and two of the best golfers in the world and a loudmouth disc jockey.

The basic idea was simple. Any pro could challenge Palmer and Player to a match, and the deal was good for thirteen weeks, which was all it lasted. But it was a creditable series. Arnie now owns the rights to it, and I hear they're showing it overseas.

"I see you as a Greek chorus," Irving says to me in his offices at Universal. "We want you to open and close the show, and we'll just have your voice over the action during the match."

Naturally, I wanted to be on camera more. And, besides, I was ad-libbing the fool thing. And when I wasn't ad-libbing on the course, I was ad-libbing at Universal on a soundstage next to a palm tree and a blue backdrop. "Ohhhhhh, look at *that* shot," and I wasn't even there.

But the Kid from Montana didn't arrive on the back of a flatbed truck, so I schemed a bit. After three shows, I said to myself, "What's this Greek chorus?" I went to the cameramen and told them to take more shots of me on the course—profile shots with me holding a microphone, which wasn't hooked up to anything. Imagine what the gallery thought. What is that idiot doing mouthing into a mike with no hook-up? It was all fun, of course, and I became good pals with Palmer and cleverly bootlegged a few lessons from the master.

Arnie has a fabulous sense of humor and loves to go along with a good gag, and we've developed a dandy act we pull off at Lakeside whenever he's in town. Part of his contract with United Airlines called for him to play golf with different groups at different clubs. So at Lakeside we do our act.

I tee off first and hit a bad shot, which isn't too difficult for me. Then Arnie calls me over to the side under the trees, and we do this pantomime; he's showing me the correct grip, everything. The other guys in the foursome are awestruck. Look, Whittinghill is getting a lesson from *Arnold Palmer!*

I go back and luckily, and I mean luckily, I hit a good ball the second time. Then Arnie gets up—and he's so beautiful—and hits the ball as strong and as whiplike as he always does, and it just dribbles off the tee. The other guys hide their eyes. I then take Arnie by the arm and we go off under the trees again, and I'm showing him the grip and demonstrating the swing, and the other guys mouths are agape.

And Arnie strides up and hits one of his 300-yarders—it rockets out of sight. Then everybody catches on, and they fall down. But the thing is, Arnie looks the same when he purposely dribbles one off the tee! He is so great, he can hit a bad drive with an almost perfect swing. I think of this often when I get out there and put it all together and slice one into the Los Angeles River bed.

28

Dinner with the President
(...and the belle of the ball)

One morning the Little Clown from Montana picks up the morning paper and reads an item about some local celebrities being invited to President Nixon's lavish dinner in San Diego at the Hotel Coronado. The local celebrities are Willie Shoemaker, the all-time champion jockey, and Dick Whittinghill, the local disc jockey.

DICK WHITTINGHILL!!!!!!!!!!!!!!!????????????

My name leaps out at me, I am literally stunned, as I had no idea this was going to happen.

Not only is President Nixon going to be there, but also former President Johnson and the president of Mexico. I can hardly form the words as I babble the news to Willy. "Go out and buy the most expensive dress you can find," I tell her, swelling with pride.

And this darlin' little thing looks up and me and says, "No, I'm going to make my own dress."

For the next week, Willy is making and making and making

this creation, as dedicated as Betsy Ross making the flag. The result is a stunning explosion of utter simplicity. This is a *gown*. I'm so proud. Willy wouldn't even let the stewardess hang up her dress on the flight down; she insisted on holding on to it.

Well, she looks exquisite as we enter the hotel and pass between the immaculate Naval officers with their white gloves. And it's all very elegant. Some broad from NBC is interviewing the women, and she starts talking with Willy. And they're doing five minutes!

"What was that all about," I ask.

"My gown," Willy says, her eyes sparkling.

Whoever it was couldn't believe that Willy had designed and made her own gown for the president's dinner when all these lah-dee-dah society ladies were wearing things made by Dior and all that stuff.

During the dinner we sat with Rudy Vallee and his wife and a southern senator, whose wife finally ordered bourbon, bless her heart, and whose husband kept trying to cop a feel on Willy.

29

The President at Lakeside
(...and the bumbling loudmouth)

Even after the dinner at Coronado, I hadn't met the President and when I learned he was going to play golf with Hope, Fred MacMurray and Jimmy Stewart at Lakeside, I grabbed my daughters and headed for the club.

"You only meet a president once in a lifetime," I told them, and they were properly excited and proud.

We're standing in a crowd of people, and old Whit is wearing a jumpsuit (a class act, as always) and more excited than his daughters. Hope is escorting Mr. Nixon and his entourage toward the clubhouse when Bob spots me. "Come here, Whit," he commands.

So Dinkpuss from Montana lurches out of the assemblage and meets the president and gets so tongue-tied, I'm embarrassing myself. "Humma-humma, uuurgh, uh, hah-hah-uummph, Mr. President, and these are my daughters, Willy and Nora." And he was so kind, and they were thrilled.

Later in the locker room, the real fun began. The president

is given a locker and an honorary lifetime membership, and his locker is three spaces from mine in the legendary cubbyhole, which is now the Hall of Fame as far as I'm concerned.

Now the scene includes George Gobel and Norm Blackburn. And Gobel is joking about calling Alice and saying he'll be a little late because he's having a drink with the president of the United States.

George says, "And she'll say, 'Yes, he's a nice man, but don't get drunk with him and ruin our evening.' "

This gets a hearty laugh from President Nixon. Whereupon, the President of the United States says to Gobel: "Why don't you call Alice, and I'll talk to her?" We're all slapping our sides as George blinks, realizing that Mr. Nixon is serious, so he calls Alice. There's some mumbling, because George is afraid of what Alice might say.

Well, the President explains that George is going to be a little late, but that he's sending her a golf ball with his name on it. Alice was pleased and stunned.

As the president left, Gobel says, "I wish he hadn't told Alice about the ball, I was going to give it to a broad in New York." Everyone collapses. And Blackburn runs out to tell Mr. Nixon what Gobel said. Later, when the president is going out the door, he leans over to Gobel and whispers, "Don't worry, George, here's another ball for that broad in New York."

30

I Never Learn
(...contests and bacchanals)

Years ago I went along with radio contests and gimmicks even though I think that contests are a cheap way to get a rating. However, if they're truly creative I suppose they have merit. We had one going where I would actually become a babysitter for a night for the lucky couple who won that week. Fortunately, this gimmick only lasted a few weeks, but imagine anyone letting a stranger into their home to take care of their children! Would *you* do it? Well, I've never been arrested on a morals charge, and the Kid from Montana has been called cuddly by a few matrons. So they probably thought I was fairly safe.

But it was a real experience, especially the first one. I drive over to the couple's house, a nice place in the San Fernando Valley, and they're practically waiting at the door, all dressed up. There's a fast introduction. They tell me the kid's in bed, and they're off like a couple of racehorses. I don't even know the kid's name or where the bathroom is, or what time the parents are coming back. Well, I find the little fellow in the sack, and he's about a year old. And his nose is running, and he's got the croup!

Now I'm calling Willy to find out what to do and writing everything down, and the little fellow is snotting all over me. And he's crying, and I'm singing to him and changing his diapers, etc.

The others were older and decidedly easier, and all this morning man from KMPC had to do was read them stories and feed their faces. Oh, by the way, the first couple. Real folks. They didn't even say thank you.

I actually forget what I said to start this other fiasco, but it had something to do with the way I kissed off Columbus Day one morning, throwing the line away that nobody really celebrated it.

The next thing I know three very heavy (not in poundage) Italian friends show up in the studio at about 7:30 A.M. Paul Caruso, the sly Sicilian attorney from Beverly Hills, is a regular listener since he's up at 6 A.M. and usually in his office by 8:00, and he calls me almost daily on the private line. He has in this short span organized a Columbus Day party. And I, of course, become the host.

Caruso brings along plenty of red wine, salami, lasagna, cheese, and garlic bread—and also Bud Furillo, then sports editor of the *Herald-Examiner*, and big John Ferraro, the former USC football star and a city councilman. My stomach wasn't ready for the salami or pasta. But the Dago Red was flowing like the Mississippi, and we were having a splendid time. Before it's over we're singing "O Solo Mio" and playing Sinatra and Como records, and people are running in from other offices lapping up the wine like peasants. The engineers are singing, too, and the secretaries are dancing. It looked like a scene from *Carmen*.

Well, then all the other ethnic groups are asking for equal

time on their special days, and I'm giving it to them—Cinco de Mayo, Bastille Day, Chinese New Year, all of them. I'm eating Mexican food and guzzling Mexican beer, French food and champagne, chow mein and whatever it was that the Chinese drink, Greek food and ouzo, and I think it was the ouzo that did it.

Ouzo is the famous Greek drink and it has a sock like Marciano. You're on the ropes before you know it is hitting you. By now, people are tuning in wondering how I'm going to finish these shows, and I don't remember what I'm saying half the time. I came out of my booth on my hands and knees after the ouzo adventure, and that's when I ran up the white flag. There were too many holidays ahead, and it was time to halt the parties before Stan Spero sent me a memo.

31

Whittinghilling for Charity

For several years now, I've been fortunate to have my name on the biggest one-day charity tournament in America. After you pay your $250 entry fee, it's the only charity golf tournament I know of where you don't pay for anything. It is held at Los Alamitos, and the late Frank Vessels (and now Milly Vessels) donates the course and the dining terrace and the food and booze at Los Alamitos Race Course, where the quarter horses run. In 1975 we raised $42,000 for charity.

The tournament is always packed with celebrities. Tim Conway, Jack Carter, Jack Lemmon, Jerry West, Jim Murray, John McKay, and a lot of good amateur golfers. And one of the nicer aspects of it is the airline stewardesses from Continental and United who serve as hostesses with each foursome.

The first year we had the tournament, there were the usual problems, especially since we were staying at an old motel near the track. We had to provide shower facilities for the stewardesses, so the men agreed to take an old double-decker bus down to the local naval training base, where they'd all shower in this big community shower. I was bidding the boys on the bus good-bye, when I noticed two stewardesses climbing aboard, and I started shouting for them to stop. Later at dinner, I asked what happened with the stewardesses?

"We didn't say anything till we got there," one of the guys said. "But when they found out we were all there to shower, they said 'what the hell' and jumped right in with us!" Gee, what good sports.

After the tournament, the awards are given out, and everyone begins eating and drinking and betting on the horses. And I swear it seems like everyone makes money because there's a lot of jumping up and down and laughing.

KMPC and Stan Spero devote a month of commercial plugs for it, but the checks actually start coming in the day after I announce the tournament date—even if I announce it in January for July. It's so popular, we have a waiting list.

We've got a few guys who want to donate $250 just to come to the party. And we had one guy offer $500 just to take a shower with the stewardesses.

32

The Dirty Old Engineers

I've had only three engineers in twenty-five years at KMPC
—old Hal Bender, crazy Larry Miller, and dirty Bob Maryon.
Bender, who's retired and living in Oregon, was very grouchy
and getting along in years when I became the morning man.
He wouldn't do much, never smiled, and sort of grunted while
he chewed on his pipe for the entire program.

Then I'd kid him a lot and call him the "Gray Fox," and
gradually he became a star. And bank tellers and grocery
clerks would say, "You're *the* Hal Bender?"

All of a sudden, it completely changed his life, took ten years
off him. He wore sloppy old clothes in the beginning, and
when he became a star, he began wearing suits and bow ties
and would laugh at everything I did and worked hard on the
program, keeping on his toes.

I'll never forget Bender at the KMPC Christmas parties. The
more he'd drink, the redder his nose got, and he became quieter
with every belt. When Bender finally fell asleep, someone would
put a napkin over his head, traditionally ending the party.

Larry Miller, still with the station, came along next and he was and is a wild man, really funny and a very good engineer whose timing is excellent.

Every morning at 8:00 when Howard Flynn comes on with the news, followed by the stock report and the sports, I go out for breakfast and read the trade papers during my half-hour break. My routine is simple and always the same—steak and sliced tomatoes.

Well, for awhile there, Miller would go up on the roof at KMPC and barbecue my steak on a charcoal grill he brought from home. He'd get the coals going between records. This went along perfectly for months until it rained one day. So Miller brought the barbecue down and fired it up in the hallway near the back delivery entrance, and everything was fine.

Now I'm ready for my half-hour break, and Larry is going for the steak when all hell breaks loose. We hear fire engines and yelling and a lot of noise out back. And Larry slides back the door, and here are a bunch of firemen with hoses and axes. Apparently, the charcoal grill had sent quite a stream of smoke through the door. I could just hear someone phoning Gene Autry and telling him Whittinghill has just burned down KMPC.

Bob Maryon is as fast as any of them, and his timing is perfect, too. He's using as many wild voice tracks as we ever did, maybe more, but his timing is so right you don't notice it. And it's perfect for me because he knows when to hit me with one and break me up. And nothing sounds funnier on radio than a natural break-up.

I've used the engineers as the foils for most of the ethnic jokes I've told on the air, substituting engineer for the ethnic term.

Q: How many engineers does it take to change a light bulb?
A: One to hold the bulb and three to turn him.

Q: How many engineers does it take to rob a bank?

A: Five. Two to make the stick-up and three to write the note.

Q: Why is the suicide rate so low among engineers?

A: Who can get killed jumping out a of basement?

Remember, always be nice to your engineer or he can cut you off and then——

33

Did You Whittinghill This Morning? (...and "The Romance of Helen Trump")

Behind every great advertising campaign sits one man. Only an idea can make it work; no sales staff or computer in the world can make it work without an idea man.

Sitting like a pudgy elf on the second floor of KMPC is John Asher, vice president in charge of public relations. His humor is so "in" at times even I don't understand it. In fact, most of the time, I don't understand John, who is operating on a wavelength no one else hears. I've been on the golf course when Asher is holding private conversations with himself and laughing under his breath. But please don't take him away—we need him, whatever he does!

One day several hundred ratings ago, Asher catches me in the hallway and says, "What do you think of this as a billboard and ad campaign?"

On a sheet of paper was written: "DID YOU WHITTING-HILL THIS MORNING?"

I told him I thought it was the greatest thing I ever heard of.

Think of it, taking a long last name and making a verb out of it! Of course, it was a smash hit. It was on billboards and the back of buses all over town and everybody took it differently. We received letters from listeners who said they "Whitting-hilled" in the cars, local parks, bathrooms, in beds, airplanes, trains, boats, haylofts, kitchens, and even in a few bars. And the other great aspect of it was that people who didn't listen to my program were now tuning in to find out what it meant.

Along about the same time, impish Asher comes up with another gem, a satire of all soap operas called "The Romance of Helen Trump." The last of the network soaps had perished, and it was the perfect moment to launch a daily spoof.

Helen Trump, we soon discovered, was a warm and wonderful woman, with big knockers, who was all things to all men. It was a delight in double entendre and the press ate it up, which is one sure way to determine a rating.

We used a corny, typical soap opera theme, and I'd narrate her latest romantic escapade. The playlet always closed with Helen's lastest lover heavily breathing promises to his pulsating sweetheart. The names of her lovers were so double entendre, even Page of *The Times* was selective in printing them. But by today's radio standards, when they can say the ultimate four-letter expletive on those gross FM stations, our naughty material was and is only naughty.

"Helen Trump" enjoyed a long run on KMPC until we were forced to shelve it because our new general manager, a humorless guy who was not liked by many, ordered it off the air because it was too dirty. Besides, I don't think he ever *got* any of it.

Funny, also around the same time, we lost the newsman, John Babcock, who did all the voices of Helen's lovers. Today they are done by newsman Howard Flynn, my old program director.

But Helen, that great old broad, who I secretly fell in love with, went out in a blaze of newsprint. The *Los Angeles Examiner* gave her a six-column obit: "HELEN TRUMP WALKS OUT ON WHITTINGHILL." *The Times*, always more conservative, gave it a column of sad regrets without a splashy headline. Herewith the final episode* as John Asher wrote it:

THEME: (Establish and fade under)

DICK: Around the corner and up your street, we bring you another chapter . . . in fact, the last chapter, in THE ROMANCE OF HELEN TRUMP, a chapter entitled: "She's Afraid to Walk the Streets at Night, So She's Looking for Another Profession." Yes, another profession . . . marriage. For only yesterday Helen received a proposal from the Handsome Stranger. He was the first man in years to propose something Helen could do standing up. And so the wedding bells are chiming . . . and you and I are losing a warm and wonderful friend. As for Helen, she is parting from the host of friends she has made through the years. Men like Bowden G. Bumtosser, a man who drinks so much that Esso has bought offshore drilling rights to his liver. And her oldest friend, Rufus von Mittlesniffer, the nuclear physicist who invented a car that would run on prune juice. It worked just fine but it had to make far too many stops. Farewell, too, to Stevo Studstacker. What a loser! The other day he fell off the Santa Monica pier and someone else's life passed before his eyes. How can Helen forget Charley Musclecramp? Rather easily. You see, Charley tried to pose for the centerfold in a girly magazine . . . only to find that his center had folded several years ago. Ah, but now, let us stand aside as Helen comes down the center aisle. What a vision she is. The neckline of her gown is as low as the law of gravity could make it. But why not? After all, it's Helen's wedding and she has a perfect right. And a darn good left, too. As Helen draws closer to the altar, she becomes more and more animated. Is it emotion? Or is her living bra doing push ups? Can it be that she is afraid to put her life into the hands of the Handsome Stranger? No, after all, Helen has bought insurance that gives her blanket coverage. It covers anything that happens under a blanket. Ah, but let us hush now . . . for at this moment the Handsome Stranger is lifting Helen's veil. Yes, their marriage is being sealed with a searing kiss. And in this sacred moment a strangled cry is heard from the back of the church.

HOWARD: Oh, Helen! Helen! Helen! Farewell, sweetest of all creatures. Farewell for ever! (Sobs)

MUSIC: (The Wedding Recessional)
           END

*Copyright © 1958 John Asher.

I now realize that Helen Trump was the single most popular feature our modest stock company ever produced over KMPC. In the ten years between front office regimes, old Whit was continually bombarded with requests to bring back the wonderful old broad. Despite my philosophy that once you've done it, don't repeat it, I have to confess I wanted to bring her back, too.

So, when our present vice-president and general manager, Stanley L. Spero, took over for Mr. Humorless (whom, incidentally, I always got along with), we reinstated "The Romance of

Helen Trump," which is better than ever, according to the
faithfuls.

Judge for yourself. Herewith a recent chapter* of the new
adventures of Ms. Trump—all things to all men:

THE ROMANCE OF HELEN TRUMP   Episode 349

THEME: (Establish and fade under)
DICK: Around the corner and up your street, we
                bring you another chapter in THE RO-
                MANCE OF HELEN TRUMP, a chapter
                entitled: "When She Advised Him to Ride
                Bareback He Started to Take His Pants Off."
                A day of gloom. Even the very atmosphere is
                saturated by a sense of despair. And alas,
                Helen is caught in the cold grip of remorse.
                Her past appears to be a barren landscape
                littered with ruins. And the present . . .
                well, there's a number of ruins in that, too.
                Ma Crunchknuckle called her last night. She
                was wearing a new deodorant. It was called,
                "Janitor in a Drum." When she entered
                Helen's house the mice jumped on chairs.
                Later, Helen was disturbed to find that Ma
                was knitting a whip while she read, "The Joy
                of Sex." Still, Ma had some good news. She
                had bought a new home. On a clear day she
                can see Catalina. The home is in Avalon.
                When Ma left, the Handsome Stranger
                dropped in. Helen couldn't remember his
                face but his hands were certainly familiar.
                Still, his kisses really made her sit up and
                open her eyes. Usually, kisses had the oppo-
                site effect. All too soon Helen discovered that
                the Handsome Stranger was not in the best

of health. Dr. Peter Proctor, an odds and
ends man, had charged him fifty dollars and
told him he'd just have to live with it. A lot of
good that advice did. It was like having a
hooker tell you to take cold showers. When
the Stranger left, Rufus dropped by. The fool
asked Helen if he could steal a kiss. What a
dummy! If he had only known it, he had a
chance to steal a Cadillac and he had settled
for a hubcap. Well, there was just no way to
figure Rufus. Who else would write a book
called *Jonathan Livingston Fruitfly*? Ah, but
let us set aside dull care for at this very moment someone is mounting Helen's steps,
crossing her stoop, reaching for her knocker.
Let's step aside and listen.

HOWARD: Oh, Helen! Helen! How desirable you are!
How tempting! Yes, how deeply stirring!
Oh, I wish my wife was like you . . . provocative, accommodating. But all she wants to
do is go to movies . . . movies that are either
about sex or disaster. Why, Helen, with me
they're the same thing!

THEME: (Up and out)
           END

*Copyright © 1975 John Asher.

Ah, Helen, ah, John, ah, Howard. We're just three naughty
nymphs in the commercial jungle, paled by discussions of oral
copulation and SLA bulletins on listener-supported and FM
underground stations.

And then there's the entertainment critic in town who claims
to be my friend who has said he'd like to blow the whistle on me

for getting so dirty. And he reviewed "Deep Throat" and satirized it, not really condemning it. We're a bit naughty (not dirty), and he takes us seriously.

Whittinghill, you're getting serious; this is supposed to be a madcap adventure.

34

Willy and Nora

.

What kind of offspring would come out of a liason between a loudmouth disc jockey and a former "Miss England" from Montana? Willy and Nora Whittinghill. Two delightful, lovely children who have been a joy to their parents and have a little of old dad and old J.N. in them, too. Their charm and love for all things comes directly from their mother.

Willy, especially, loves the little creatures. Nora does, too, but is allergic to anything furry. Willy, now twenty-one, recently adopted a little squirrel we found, apparently orphaned, and it is now a household pet, completely domesticated through her ingenious touch.

It reminds me of little Nora's desperate search for a pet that wouldn't give her a rash or cause those sneezing fits. When she was small, she loved animals and was dying to touch them and couldn't, and I felt so sorry for her. Finally, I decided I'd find her a pet even if she had to put *me* on a leash. So we went to pet shop after pet shop, with my little Nora tagging along, looking for something that wouldn't make her sick.

One owner went all out. "I got it!" he finally said, triumphantly after we'd seen everything from ants to aardvarks. And he trots out a Mexican hairless. Of course, why hadn't I thought of it. This dog was hairless. But right away, Nora starts coughing and wheezing. We were depressingly silent in defeat. No pet for little Nora.

"Wait a minute," the owner bubbled, as if he'd just sold out the store. "There's nothing in the store, except *one* thing," he said, raising an index finger and giving us a wink. And, thank God, Nora loved it right away, just crazy about it.

"What did you get her?" my wife said, just thrilled to pieces.

We showed her and my wife nearly fainted. I got Nora a boa constrictor. It was the only thing she could touch. She loved it and she named it "Pinky."

Guardedly, we kept it for awhile, but I guess I was a little cruel, because I could see this thing becoming nine feet long and swallowing the house. Well, you're supposed to force-feed these snakes, but I didn't tell Nora. And she would make little hamburger balls and place them by the boa constrictor, and this stupid thing would just look at them; he didn't know how to eat them. About a month later, he died.

Both of these kids were fast of mind, especially Willy when she was around eight or nine. At this tender age, I taught Willy how to play poker, blackjack, and craps. We had jolly evenings together in our Little Las Vegas in North Hollywood.

One morning after the program, my wife calls me at the station.

"You had to go and do it, didn't you?"

"What do you mean?" I stammered, recognizing that tone in her voice.

"You had to teach Willy how to shake dice."

"Yeah, so?" I said.

"You better come home, she's running a floating crap game in the neighborhood."

Sure enough, out in the garage darlin' little Willy was

cleaning out all her friends of their weekly allowance. The mothers were calling Willy, Sr., protesting, "Little Margie just came home asking for another quarter. What is going on over there?"

35

A Halloween Memory

When Willy and Nora were very little, about four and five, I took them out for their first official Halloween trick or treat— around the old neighborhood where everybody knew everybody.

We dressed them up as little devils: horns, tails, tiny wooden pitchforks. They were adorable. Since I knew everyone, I escorted my little devils on their festive tour. I'd take them up to the front of the houses, then sneak around in back into the kitchens and have a couple of quick shooters with the parents. And this continued on all through the neighborhood.

About three hours later, I'm carrying a small glow, and I've momentarily lost Willy and Nora, my little devils. Finally, I see these two devils and grab them by the arm and commence to march them off to home, and they've had so much fun and their sacks are full and they're crying and protesting— "No, no!"

And I'm literally dragging them home, becoming very

irritated. "You can't act up like this," I say, "you've had a good night's trick or treat."

I get them home, fighting all the way, and take off their masks—and I've got the wrong kids! So I run them back and somehow find my own kids, who are kind of walking dazed down the block looking for their stupid father.

36

My Darlin' Wilamet

I've always detested self-indulgence in public, and maybe that's why it's hard for me to write a book. But at the same time I'm being self-indulgent every morning on radio.

A few deejay's think they are so great—it's no big deal being one; it doesn't require having a lot of talent. It's only a peculiar ability. It's having a peculiar ability, and that's what I believe —I have a peculiar ability. Perhaps the only advantage I have over those less peculiar is I know something about music, so I offer something besides that which "has a nice beat."

Now, let me be self-indulgent about my wife, the former Wilamet Matson, whom I met at the University of Montana and thought she wore too much makeup. But I couldn't think of anyone else but her since then. After school was out, we both came to Hollywood; old Whit went to dramatic school, and she went to Bud Murray's School of Dance. We both were intent on having a *career*. During this time, we saw each other almost every day, but being poor, marriage was not imminent.

Somehow, Wilamet got involved in something called the "Miss America Exhibit" in San Diego, and faithful old Whit wasn't going to let her go, so I visited her down there to keep an eye on her. She was appearing as "Miss England." It was the darndest thing. All the girls were mounted in glass cages, and at certain times every hour, one of them would be showcased to the public.

So, I'm standing there one day, very proud, and the announcer says, "Now, ladies and gentlemen, here is Miss England," and here comes Willy in the glass cage. She looked wonderful, with a beautiful body. And I'm standing there beaming, and a little nervous and a lot jealous, and there are two sailors behind me and they're beaming, too.

"Holy cow!" one of them says, "how'd you like to bang *that?!*"

Well, I turned around and let fly on this guy—gave him a helluva punch—and there's a big scene, and the guy who ran the show kicked me out and banned me from the place.

We went back to Helena for a vacation, Miss England and I, and in the Parrot restaurant I proposed, and Willy said yes. We got in the car and I went through two or three stoplights, singing all the way to mom and dad's house. We burst in the door, and I babbled out the news to dad! I'll never forget the look on his face. Then it sank in—I didn't have a job, and this was old J.N. I was talking to.

Anyway, the Kid from Montana and Miss England were married on that unforgettable vacation back home, and the reception was a memorable affair. My old man was kicking up his heels pretty good, even though we were married in the *Catholic* church. And Willy's father, an agnostic, was looking around in amazement, even peeking in the confessionals.

Oh, it was a jolly time, and when we prepared to set out on our honeymoon, I'll never forget Dad's advice, and by this time I think my dad thought I was going off to college.

"Son," he said, "there is one thing I always want you to remember: Keep your peter in your pants."

Willy and I took a bus all the way back to Los Angeles, and you should have seen the low-lifes that got on. Bad breath, dirty smelling feet. And when we got to Butte, Montana, it was even worse. Butte was the toughest town in the West. The welcome wagon was a tank, and the high school paper was the only school paper in the country that had an obituary section.

These people were playing guitars and screaming and smelling, and I knew Willy couldn't survive it, so I told her to stretch out on the very back seat and pretend she was sick. I threw a coat over her and warned people away—and we had the rear of that putrid bus to ourselves all the way home.

Soon afterward, my darlin' Willy gave me the real first indication of what an innocent child she was, and, always will be, thank God. On our first Thanksgiving together, she slaved all day—before asking for help. It was taking too long, she thought. It should have. She was stuffing the bird through its beak.

And just recently, she confirmed her blithe spirit when I encouraged her to come into the living room and watch the absolutely sensational football game between UCLA and USC. You must understand, until this point last year, my darlin' Willy had never watched a football game on TV!

Just as she sat down, a UCLA back swept wide to the right and ran out of bounds, knocking a press photographer head over heels.

"That's terrible, that's awful!" Willy shrieked. "Why did he do *that*?

I explained it was just a freak thing. Then, ABC played it back on Instant Replay, which Willy had never seen. The UCLA running back hits the photog from a different angle.

"Dick, he did it again—how brutal! How can you watch such a thing?!"

(Say good night, Gracie.)

Last year, I went back to Helena and visited the Parrot, where I proposed to Willy and the same booth is there, and, so help us, the same waitress is working there. After all these years. You're wrong Thomas Wolfe—you *can* go home again.

37

The Next Twenty-five Years

Our adventure together was decidedly shorter than twenty-five years on the air, and light years shorter than the beginnings in Montana. But I like keeping it short; just the best highlights of the best moments.

Why have I lasted this long? Who knows? Maybe it's because I'm honest, and people know I am. Maybe too damn honest. But this is the way I am. I still believe that missing mass is a sin. And I still believe in people and love my country.

And I've had acceptance. I never thought I'd last this long against the competition. It really amazes me. Old Whit enjoys his work, and I have a delightful time laughing and giggling and kidding people. And the listeners accept me and what they hear *is* me.

I base everything on humor and people ask me what do I see that's different in humor these days. First of all, let's establish the fact that I may be humorous, but I'm no comedian. What has changed? Basically, we're more permissive, but on the other hand, we don't do ethnic jokes or stories. The basis of all good humor was ethnic, clear back before vaudeville. Now everyone is too uptight and sensitive. But people will still laugh when you put yourself down, and I do that naturally.

Philosophy? I don't know if I have one—I'm still scared after all these years. I'm no superstar; I simply have a peculiar ability, I guess I'm a peculiar person. Whatever I've achieved in life I owe to my wife, the greatest mother, truly a one-man woman. I don't know where or what I'd be without her.

All right, audience—and the guy who wants to take my pulse everyday—when is this little Kid from Montana going to retire?

When I don't enjoy it anymore and I'll know when that happens. Or maybe those mysterious ratings will catch up with me someday, and I'll be gone. Until then, I'll enjoy being part of whatever that critic meant by "the culture."

Thank you very much for listening.

Now, if you'll excuse me . . .

Index

149